This book is dedicated to

mum and dad

My shelter from the storm of life

my comfort when it rained,

my sunshine, my respect

I worked with Terry Lawless in Dagenham Docks many moons ago, and to be honest, to my knowledge, Terry had never set foot on the bravest stage of all, which without doubt is the boxing ring. Terry went on to manage 4 world champion boxers, in my opinion it should have been 5, as he also managed my favourite boxers ever Jimmy Batten. I am pleased to say Jimmy is a great friend, which is just as well, with a boxing record like his you would not want to be his enemy. Born in a tough area of Millwall he started boxing at 6 years of age before turning professional in 1974.

Jimmy's amateur career was second to none. He won 3 national schoolboys titles and 2 ABA titles going unbeaten for an incredible 5 and a half years. I watched most of his professional fights and was delighted to see him win the British Light Middle Weight Championship from Albert Hillman in 1977 at the Royal Albert Hall, he was just 21 years of age. He went on to have 49 professional fights winning 21 by KO. When Jimmy retired in 1983 he entered my world, the world of show business, and I was pleased to see him secure many acting rolls in film and TV, including 'The Bill' and working alongside the Kemp brothers in the award- winning film 'The Krays' But he really shone when working the pubs and clubs of his very own East End as a comedian and singer.

4

He has proved to be a big draw and you can guarantee a full house wherever jimmy plies his trade. Whilst Jimmy has a great singing voice it's great to hear some of those stories he tells between his songs.

All I can say Jimmy is all the very best for the future and thanks for those wonderful memories;

You are one knock out of a bloke

Jimmy Jones

In my long and adventurous life. I have met all sorts of people. Jimmy Batten is one of the people I am so glad I met and extremely proud of our cherished friendship. He is the nicest guy in the world who remains a credit to his craft of boxing.

Former British Featherweight Champion

Sammy Mc Carthy

8

I first met Jimmy Batten at Millwall Youth Football club, we were 11 years old. Jimmy is a diamond. To some he could be a rough diamond, especially if you were his opponent in the ring. He was, and still is, the life and soul of the party.

We were in a boxing tournament London v Lancashire in 1972. I was fighting a guy called Fir and he was fighting a boxer called Shaw. They were both schoolboy champions. Jimmy said to me "we should go up to them both and tell them we are going to knock them out"

I told him we were not allowed to do that, but he did not care he went up to his opponent eye to eye and said; "I am going to knock you out" It must have had an effect because that's exactly what Jimmy done. 50 years later it still makes me smile and I am proud to say Jimmy is still a special friend.

 Former WBC World Flyweight Champion

Charlie Magri

Jimmy Batten first met me in the Royal Oak pub Canning Town London with his manager Terry Lawless. Within a few minutes I was laughing. He is such a funny guy every time I see him I cannot help but smile. Jimmy always looks good and smells good. He would be the life and laughter at any party. But beneath those smiles is a dedicated serious man who was unbeaten for many years. Winning the Lonsdale belt outright

At the time, he was challenging for the world welterweight title, there was a lot of good boxers fighting at that weight. That said, Jimmy is, and always will be, first class. If I had to describe him in a few words I would say he is a survivor. Whatever life throws at him he faces the challenge with defiance and a smile. We met recently, and although the years have taken their toll on us both, within a few minutes of shaking his hand we were laughing, just like we did back in the day. Proud to know him, honoured to call him a friend.

Former world heavyweight Champion

Frank Bruno

I have known Jimmy Batten since he entered the boxing scene in the East End of London at the age of 12, where he won the 'National Championships' year after year. Unbeaten for many years he turned Pro under the same manager, Terry Lawless, as me. We both trained at the famous boxing gym The Royal Oak in Canning Town. We have spared hundreds of rounds together and became close friends. He helped me win the European Welterweight title in Paris in 74 and the World Welterweight title in Mexico City in 75. I spared with Jimmy when he became the British Light Middleweight Champion in 77. When he fought the great Roberto Duran he took him ten rounds and was very unlucky not to get the decision against what is considered one of the greatest boxers of all time. He remains one of my best boxing buddies and stable mate. We spent years together sharing such fabulous times. A really 'down to earth' guy who I have the utmost respect for.

Former European and World Welterweight Champion.

John H Stracey

Round One seconds out

St Andrews Hospital Bow London 1955

The hospital started life in 1871 as the Popular Asylum.

Built next door to the Stepney Workhouse that provided many of its inmates.

It was a year of change, the start of the Vietnam war and race riots in the US and me taking my first big breath of London smog. Friday the 7th of November, I started life, to become part of a large group of close knit families that scraped a living on the Isles of Dogs. It was in fact in two parts one half was Cubit Town the other half Millwall. Home was with my mum's parents in a small house that would now need to shuffle about to make room for the 7th member of their family. The towns were linked by a wooden footbridge.

It took just a few minutes on foot to get to the other side, by bus you would need to go right around the Island and take up to an hour. Most families on the Island were large and skint (poor). But we never felt we were poor as everyone we knew had the same or less than us. Our play ground was the bombsites left by the blitz. Our part of London, close to the docks, took the biggest and most frequent air raids Hitler could send out. But our family got through, there was a saying back then; if the doodle bugs (flying bomb) has got your name on it there was sod all you could do to change it.

It was that defiant spirit that was in my genetic make-up.

Jimmy age 2 years with sister Eileen and brother Tony London 57

You may win some you may lose some, but you never backed down. Fighting was in my blood. The bomb sites would see a big gang of us, names like the Saints, the Buddon's, Sails and Bassets are and indelible part of my endearing memories.

Some gathering scrap wood for the fire, others going off to steal potatoes from the allotments to cook to a cinder in the red-hot ashes. We would hook these black nuggets out with a stick. The skin was so hot it would stick to your lips and cause severe pain if you did not toss them from hand to hand long enough for them to cool down. The pure white insides soon got stained by our blackened fingers, but that was all part of the magic of 'stolen fruit'. Nothing was left, even the burnt black skin was eaten. Rumour had it that it was the most nutritious part of the spud. A rumour that would be proven true many years later. Around this time whilst running 'full pelt' over the bombsite I fell, and got a toy metal car stuck in my mouth that lacerated the inside of my cheeks and roof of my mouth.

I was rushed to the doctors who managed to remove the toy before the blood blocked my airways and choked me to death. "You want to count yourself lucky Jim" the doctor said, and from then on, the nick name Lucky Jim stuck.

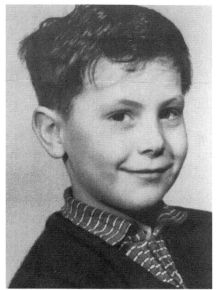

Jimmy age 7 Cubit Town London 1962

I loved school, not the academic side of it but the sports side in which I excelled. In athletics, I was always first or second, Mr Halder, the sports teacher, said I was an excellent athlete and a pain in the arse. I never did take orders very well, usually answering a request with 'Why?' was the main reason for the pain in the arse title. I was football mad and made the school team. Later, thanks to good mates David and Dennis Bodden, became part of the Millwall youth team. This would have been my future had it not been for a bug. That bug was boxing. Athletics and football, I loved, but boxing was my destiny and my life. On my 10th birthday I begged my dad to take me to the boxing club. My mum was not too keen, but my dad wanted me to be able to learn how to defend myself and, so I got my first taste, and it was a taste, I can still smell the leather and sweat that gave all boxing clubs that smell that stays in your nostrils for life. The Poplar and District Boxing Club in Roman Rd E3 was to be where I learned the ropes, and more importantly how to keep off the ropes. It was here I met men like Bert Morgan, Boxer Billy Jones and Bob Galloway. I can still hear the voice of Ronny Cooper, Olympic representative, drumming into my head; 'Balance Jimmy, left right left'. A lesson that stayed with me my whole career.

Me age 11 with some of my trophies

The Summer of 66 the Batten family went to Butlins, Clacton. I was delighted to find they ran a boxing club for the kids. As it turned out it was one of my best holidays ever. We spared for a week before we were matched to fight. I was to box a boy called, Freddy Pinner, who was a national schoolboys finalist. When he stepped into the ring I thought I had made a mistake. On his short's he wore the badges of national champion. My second saw me looking and whispered 'it 'aint the badges on your shorts that win matches but the power in your gloves. I later found out, after I held him to a draw, that they were his brothers shorts and he just wore them to make me nervous. They all said I boxed well, I could not wait for the holiday to end so I could get back to my second home at the boxing club. The official rule was you had to be 11 before getting a proper fight. Two weeks before my 11th birthday I got my first official match. The venue was East India Hall (Poplar Baths) on the 22nd October 1966. As the car pulled up outside the hall with all its red lights, and hearing the crowd inside I felt a tingle running right through my young body. I can still recall the smell of the dressing room and the, smoke filled, hall even today. I was boxing a lad called Ray Welham, from the famous Repton Boxing Club, that opened its doors in the late 1800s and is still in business today. I beat him and got the badge of honour, a black eye, to announce to all 'here is a boxer'. Telling my mates at school and bathing in the glory was a hook for Boxing that went deep and remained every sweat stained step of my career.

Extract from my journal;

26th March 1968 age 12; London Primary Schoolboy Championships, Manor Place Baths Woolworth London; I beat G Wood of Morpeth School. I stopped him in the first round, after knocking him down twice. He had a big bruised eye and was crying so the referee stopped the fight. I was in the 6st 7lb Group, but I only weighed in at 6st 4lb, they said that did not matter as I was not over the 6st 7lb mark. The press was kind to the boy I stopped as they said he lost on points but that was wrong as it did not go past the first round

Tony age 13 and me age 12

Round Two

Seconds out

That season I had 12 fights and one exhibition fight, I lost two of them but remembered who I lost to and the next season made double sure I beat them on the return match. The next

Jimmy Batten v David Coombes 16/01/69 East India Hall London

season was when I was delighted that my brother Tony started to box. He was good company on the bus from the Island to Roman road. The journey by bus and foot took about an hour but it was great to have him join me on the way to training. He went on to become a very good boxer winning the junior ABA title when he got to 15 he decided to hang up his gloves, but I continued boxing.

That year the London Schoolboy association ran a competition for those boy's too young to enter the National comp. I won that and went on to win three National titles in a row. You would need a lot of fights back then to reach the finals. You would need to be able to travel all over the country. The finals that year were in Blackpool, at Pontins Holiday Camp. It was a great big family affair, my mum and dad would come for the weekend with my Aunt Doreen and my cousins, like Ronny Farmer, would be there to cheer me on. We were very close; my cousins were like brothers and sisters. I had 15 fights and lost the last one to a boxer called Sammy Morris from Coventry, I later went on to beat him twice. That season me and Tony boxed for London Schoolboys against Lancashire spending 3 days at Lake Windemere my roommate was Martin Ridley who joined us on a boat trip across the great Lake

My Lucky Jim magic worked again just before the season started. We were all 'mucking about jumping park benches, one, with a plank missing, ended up stuck deep into my knee. For most people, it would have been a long time to get better, and it could have torn ligament ruining my career before it had hardly begun. But 'Lucky' Jim was back on the pitch, I played for the school team, and later Millwall Youth, and in the ring 2 months later. I now had a Saturday job working in the local Butchers, Alf Hugh and his son Geoff, who was 10 years older than me. It was then that

 my Dad went to prison, my mum always said it was something stupid he had done, and we were not encouraged to ask questions. But Geoff was there to take dads role and help me with my training. It was such a vulnerable time for me had Geoff not stepped onto the role I don't think my boxing would have flourished as it did. Whilst Playing for the club we had a new boy join. He seemed to me to be too small to play, but turned out to be a talented player. The next I heard of him he was boxing. The way I saw it if he was too small for football he was too small to box. His name was Charly Magri, 5ft 3 inches tall, a two-handed scrapper, managed by Terry Lawless he went on to take the aba youth flyweight crown in 72 and turning pro captured the European title in 79 and became world flyweight champ in 83. We remained in touch and are still good mates. We were soon boxing for London School's against Dublin Schools, I fought a boxer called Kevin Driskell, I won and so did my brother. The venue was Shoreditch Town Hall that that looked like an old-fashioned theatre. The next fight was abroad, by train then ferry then train again, all the way to Berlin in a separated Germany. The train had soldiers with guns we were to box in the 1936 Olympic Stadium which Hitler had been so frustrated to not only see an American win medals, but a black American defied his idea of a 'master' race.

On the train was a party of young girls, which, as with red blooded teenagers of all nationalities, occupied our thoughts more than the guns or political history. Again, me and Tony won, as did most of our group. Cheered on by the likes of J.H. Stacy, British and European and world champion and a good mate. When we got back I was expelled from school just for making a giant ice ball out of frozen snow and hitting the head master so hard it nearly knocked him out. So, I was off to Langdon Park School Poplar. I was not bad but, because I never turned down a dare, I was, looking back, probably stupid. When given good advice, I cocked a deaf one, (did not listen) getting into fights more often than getting into bed.

One fight was because a boy had the hump, (angry) because he had failed the football trials, hit me across the back of the head with a cricket bat, which would cause me problems in years to come. But luck was always around the corner for Jimmy Batten. It was now that I met my first true love Theresa Hawkins. At 13 they said, 'I did not know what love was' but I did, and I loved Theresa, whose grandparents lived a few doors away from my grandparents. We were then living at 12 Parsonage Lane Cubit Town I had trouble fitting in with the new school, it was a mixed school and the girls were a big distraction and the cause of most of the fights. Where there was fighting you could bet I would be somewhere in the middle of it all. But I soon made new friends and settled down to my new mates and seeing my girl -friend at the church hall club for kids. I began to play football for the school team around this time and soon was good enough to get a trial for Millwall. I played well and was offered to sign schoolboy forms. They wanted me to sign an apprenticeship, but I said 'no'. I was a boxer and that came first. My dad would be away in prison for about a year. How my mum coped with feeding and clothing us all was nothing short of a miracle. She worked part time at the bakers so anything that was not sold at the end of the day would be stale by the morning, so she got to bring stuff home for us. As I mentioned in round one we were, and still are, a very close family, my Aunts Doreen and Shirley 'pitched in to help mum out.

Round Three

What can't speak can't lie

It was a big blow to us all when my uncle Ron (Ronald Bender) was sent down (to prison) for 20 years with the Kray Twins for murdering Jack 'the hat' Mac Vitie in a basement flat on Evering Road, he was just 30 years old. His wife, Aunt Buddy, and her kids Ronnie Johnny and Jimmy practically moved in with us. We did not find this unusual, we always treated our cousins like brothers and as mum often said, 'family is family.

It was the evening of 28th October 1967 when it 'all came on top' (went wrong) Jack the hat was invited to the party unaware that he was about to pay for what he had not done. What he was paid to do was murder the Krays business partner Lesly Payne, the amount varies, some say a ton (£100) deposit and £400 when the job was done, others say a monkey (£500) deposit and a monkey when Payne was dead. Those that knew never said.

Whatever the amount he did not carry out the job. He travelled out to Payne's house and banged on the door with gun behind his back. Mrs Payne answered the door and told Jack Leslie was not in, and closed the door. It was then, as he travelled back, he made a decision that would cost him his life. Even though it would be obvious he did not carry out the task, he decided to keep the deposit. When he arrived at the party Reggie Kray held a gun to his head and pulled the trigger. It failed to fire, he pulled it again and the gun jammed. Picking a knife off a nearby table he stabbed Jack many times in the head and neck. Part of the gang, who were at the party, was Tony and Chris Lambrianou and my uncle Ronny Bender. Their bosses left telling the three of them to clean up the mess. They wrapped the body in an eiderdown and bundled it in to the back of Tony's car. His brother Chris and my uncle Ronny followed. What really happened to the body is only known to these 3 gang members. They have never said. The golden rule for criminal organisations, the world over, is you never talk. I was bought up on the saying 'a grass' (police informer) is worse than a thief.

Having the NABC we went on a trip to Arnhem with Joe Bugner, who had just won the title, with his manager Andy Smith and our trainer Kevin Hicky and me old mate Charlie Magri. We went around all the local attractions including the 'red light district' as a 15- year- old I learned a lot that day.

When we got back I had a fight arranged with Micky Quin, an old adversary. We had both been unbeaten for some time, so we went at it 'hammer and tongs'. The crowd loved it and roared us on. The fight was close until the third when I broke

Micky's jaw and won by a stoppage. The press lapped it up and I got more publicity, 'Jaw Breaker Batten' was the headlines and becoming a celebrity at 16, was more to do with the way I 'scrapped' than the fact I had been unbeaten for a long time.

I joined West Ham Boxing Club and began to be trained by Len Welham, who was the dad of Ray Welham my first opponent in the ring. I still had my girl Theresa, but we had our ups and downs.

From my journal;

London v Lancashire. They gave me a tie I had to give back and a badge I could keep. I beat a boxer called G Glover stopped him the first minute, he had a Gash under his eye and his nose was pouring blood. The ref stopped the fight to stop him any more punishment. I shared a room with my brother and Martin Ridley as soon as it stopped raining we went out on a boat on Lake Windemere. It rained a lot

I left school at 15, I had no Qualifications and for most that would have been difficult but once again I was Lucky. Volkswagen, who sponsored my boxing club West Ham, and had offices in Plaistow, gave me a job. It was a decent Job as were many others that followed, but I never settled. I worked as a cloth cutter, shipping clerk, working the board in a betting shop, before computers took over, window cleaner and for Bork Shipping with Peter and Brian Basterbull, which was more money than the £7 a week Volkswagen were paying me. They gave me a job filling out custom papers and taking them up the custom offices at Tower Bridge. At 16 they gave me a Lambretta, because I said I could ride one. In fact, the only time I had ever rode one was on the one the lads stole, and we ran it till it busted on the 'mud shoot' fields. Whilst Driving around the Island to see Theresa, on very icy roads, I hit a car and was sent right over its roof. To my surprise I landed on my feet without a scratch, My luck to the rescue again. I ran with the Mile End Mob, I got my brother involved for a while, but he was a lot smarter than those that got caught for petty theft and fighting. Friday night was 'boy's night' Saturday was when you see your girl. For me that was Theresa the one and only girl I wanted to be with. It was around this time I received a blow that had more effect on me than all the punches in all the fights put together. My Aunt Doreen, who I loved dearly, was killed in a car crash in Dagenham. Most of the family had moved out to Basildon. My mum asked me to phone and offer my condolences, but I found it impossible to control the sadness that fell on me like a ton of bricks I could not seem to get past the grief and began losing my way and my jobs. I must have been still wrapped up in my grief when working as a window cleaner on the roof of Vauxhall Bridge Dairy when I slipped and fell. As the ground came rushing towards me my jeans caught on a protruding bolt and stopped my fall. They had to get long ladders to get me down as I dangled from the roof. If the jeans ripped before the ladders got to me or they had not caught on the bolt I would have died instantly. But my luck was still with me. My Junior career was now over, and I had turned senior with 6 national titles and unbeaten for 5 years. Turning senior was a lot harder, I began mixing with mates like Jimmy Hodgson, Laurie Walker and Micky Browning. Running with a gang called the 'Mile End Mob' that included Joe and Paul Williams Tony Sinclair Kadie Dadsy Jacky Sawyer and many others. A pack of good mates thieving fighting and laughing about it all. But first and foremost, I am a senior boxer and needed to train to the level that would allow me to keep on winning. The fact I had not lost in such a long time meant there was plenty out there who would put in the extra training and miles on the road to take that record off me. Not everyone likes someone who keeps winning. How hard it would be come in the next fight, against a man not a boy. In this case it would be Alan Cable, whose brother, Jimmy Cable, was former British Middleweight Champion. I won the fight, record still intact.

From my journal 30th April 69 London v Dublin Shoreditch Town Hall;

Beat Kevin O'Driscol on points, televised fight, BBC commentator Reg Guttridge helped between rounds by Henry Cooper. I won the English Badge and the International badge. Later that year I boxed in Coventry for England w that was shown live on TV.

Round 4

from boy to man

After 9 wins as a senior I got a fight with Johnny Evans a 27 year- old from Epsom. This fight I lost, I felt strange and confused at not winning. I was convinced I had done enough and would win the fight. Before this fight I had let myself stray from the training and running needed to keep me on top. I had been drinking and over eating with my mates. I had hoped to be picked for the Commonwealth games, but they said I was too young. Looking back, I was probably not as clean cut as the boxers that went on to represent our country. The young fellow who was picked I had beaten previously, went on to win a silver medal, I think they picked the wrong man. Stands to reason, if he got a silver, and I was better, because I beat him, then I could have got gold. I was selected to box for London v the rest. I was to fight the ABA light middle weight champion Roger Maxwell. I weighed in at 10 stone 9lb, my opponent was much heavier and older. A soldier in his mid-20s. Thinking back I should never have boxed him, at that weight and with his record. It was a good fight and a close call, but I lost, and the taste of defeat I did not like one little bit. I continue with my ABA career, winning the north- east title. Then on to the London Trials held at Albert Hall. I had to get stuck in to more training and more roadwork around Millwall Park and the mud chute with friends Stephen Louther and his dad, who helped me a lot, learning a bit more each day. A year before the finals, got through the semis to the final, boxing as I did in the juniors. I won the first fight but got badly cut. Then, still with the cut eye, went on to box Johnny Evans. I beat Johnny comfortably but only because of Len Welham in my corner, keeping the blood from going in my eye. At the end of the fight I made doubly sure I thanked him for his help, both in my corner and at the gym. Onwards to the quarter finals in Hull. Charlie Magri was also up to box, I boxed Robbie Davis and lost on points. Davis went on to fight Roger Maxwell in the ABA finals and Maxwell, who I was due to box in last year's finals, beat him on points, Davis was a good strong puncher in last year's final, who I was due to box. I was very careful to dodge, and moving to make him miss. I had easily won on points, I knew, deep down, I had won. I had enough fights to know, before the final bell, if I had won or lost, I had done enough, when they gave it to the other boxer on points I knew it was another 'dodgy decision'. If I was disappointed last time a I had a 'dodgy' decision, this time I was very fucking angry. I decided it was time to change my direction and Go Pro. I had been going to the Royal Oak Gym where I would spar with greats like, John H Stracey and Maurice Hope. Through them I became friendly with Terry Lawless. Despite some bad reports about Terry I could only speak as I find. I found him to be a decent bloke and very fair in his dealings with my career. Theresa, went with me to Terry's house on Sunday and I signed the forms to become a professional. I felt on top of the world. I remember getting the taxi home and asking Theresa if the cab driver knew he had a professional boxer in the back of his cab. The boxing world had the opinion that, at 18, I was a bit on the young side. But Terry was a knowledgeable manager and in the beginning, was very careful with me and kept my 'feet on the ground'. I would run through Victoria Park with John H Stracey who would teach me they correct way to approach the level of training needed to be a successful Pro. I was still working the board in the betting shop and giving the betting shop most of my wages in bets. Then came my first professional fight, people were going to pay money to see me box. It was at the Royal Albert Hall June the 4th 1974 against George Salmon, I won on points. I felt so good hearing the result and the screaming of the crowd. Lots of them were friends and family, my dad had organised coaches to the fight from Millwall, even selling tickets himself to boost my support. That summer was one to remember. The furthest away from home I had been with Theresa had been, up till now, was to visit her uncle Tony in Tunbridge Wells. Her uncle was a great man and along with Len Darcey became our close friends. But now Theresa had booked a trip to Devon. To two young people from 'the smoke' it was like a whole new world. Normally, since the world cup had started in West Germany, I would be watching the football results, But, much to my, and the rest of the countries disgust, England had failed to qualify. The weather was hot, very hot, with occasional thunder storms. But for us heading down to the coast it was heaven. We sang, all the way down to Devon, our favourite was David Essex 's number one 'We Gonna Make You a Star'. And just to put the 'icing on the cake', after I came back from a run, I got a call from my manager Terry Lawless saying he had got me on the 'John Conteh World Title Challenge'. A momentous year 74, I got to go on the bill with the great man himself. He of course, boxed last against Jorge Victor Ahumada and won every round except one which he drew. Taking the World Light Heavyweight Title on points. I boxed against Brian Gregory of Doncaster, winning over 6 rounds on points.

Dave Cortney, Charlie Kray and Jimmy Batten

I met a guy called Greg Stein in Monte Carlo at a stopover in Paris we bumped into each other again. He was traveling with Charley Kray the twins elder brother. My family were not happy with the twins. They did not provide any of the legal help they had themselves at the trial. This was bad for the co- accused as they were left to 'hang out to dry'. Being found guilty of the much lesser crime of moving a body and preventing it being lawfully buried. Uncle Ron still got 20 years as the justice system wanted to make an example. Being linked to the twins the rough hand of justice slapping them down would also include the lesser members of the firm. The papers, the police and the public loved it. My uncle Ron, and my parents were pissed off with the 'firm' because when the 'shit hit the fan' they just looked after themselves. Honour among thieves only exists if it's not your neck in the noose. So, thinking back, it probably was not one of my best decisions the agree to go and visit Ronny Kray in Broadmoor Prison. It was a strange and gigantic place full of background noise. Like the calling of distant jungle animals, mixed with iron door slams and what sounded like metal trays being thrown on the floor. The smell is more difficult to describe, the most overpowering smell was that of a dusty charity shop mixed with Dettol antiseptic and a feint, but distinct smell, of piss. The area where we met in a common room was relaxed and watched by a male nurse who stayed in the background.

Ronny told me there was talk of a film and felt I should play the part of him, after I told him about my acting lessons and speech therapy sessions. Of course, I was recognised. When I returned I was contacted by the British Boxing Board of Control. They told me, in no uncertain terms, that if I continued to have contact with the Krays they would take away my licence. I explained the trip was not planned we were just traveling on the same plane at the same time, and I was just being polite. They accepted that and told me to be more careful in the future.

On the 28th of June 1975, I got married to my Theresa at the, SS Mary and Joseph Catholic church E14. My best man was Jimmy Hodgson. It was a great wedding with guests like Terry Lawless John H Stacey, and heavy weight champion, John L Gardener. We moved in with Teresa's parents for a while and I got myself a job on a local building site. We then moved to our first home. A small flat in Goodwill House Popular high street. That summer I won ten straight fights, my new wife did not like boxing, but she supported my dreams. What she did not like more, was me going out with my 'shady' mates and coming home messed up, or hyper. Her fears turned out to be right, although I had won the last three fights I still liked hanging about with my mates. It was when I was with them collecting ticket money in the Globe, a fight broke out. As always, when it all kicked off (when a fight began) I had to be in on the action. Someone hit my left wrist with a glass, or something sharp, as it cut the tendons in my hand, which looked like it was hanging off. The London Hospital operated that night. I was in so much pain they had to overdose me with tranquilisers over- night, they could not give any more, so I had a cloth put in my mouth, to bite down on to help me cope with the pain. after 6 weeks, they took the plaster off and my hand. It had shrunk so much I did not recognise it as being my hand. I had to attend classes to strengthen what was left of my hand. It was not useable when took on my next fight. Peter Cain was fighting at middle weight, a weight I am not used to.

He won in the 8th, why I was boxing so soon and at a weight I was not comfortable with? I don't know. My only excuse is the bug that nags me to box as many, and as often as I can. The audience were convinced that I had won, and so did I, and began to riot. One of them my mates was trying to get in the ring shouting the ref had deliberately held up the wrong hand, I stopped him. I also felt I had won, I felt the ref tighten his grip on my wrist and was sure he was going to lift my arm and declare me the winner. But he did not. Peter also felt he had done enough to win it. Whether my mate that jumped in the ring and accused the ref of deliberately putting up the wrong hand was right or wrong I don't know, or if the ref had taken a bung? (bribe) who knows, what I do know is that was the last refereeing job that ref ever done. But that bad fight, and my bad hand, soon were pushed back in my lists of important things. Apart from my good mate John H Stracey winning the world title, my beautiful first-born boy Tony was born. I remember the details as if it was an hour ago. Theresa had gone to the hospital with her mum and dad. I went on to set up my market stall. When the word came my good mate, Laurie, took over the stall as I ran all the way to maternity. I had, in my life, been in many fights. Some were life threatening. Only Last year I had been stabbed in the back and hit with a piece of wood across the head. All those scrapes were nowhere near as important as running to reach my wife before she gave birth to our first born. I got there in time for my boy's birth. At 4pm, weighing in at 6lb 4 ounces, Anthony James Batten arrived. When they gave me the baby to hold I nearly shit myself, I was shaking so much Theresa's mum took over. I remember thinking, this little boy is mine, and it is my job to protect him. My dad told me It was time for me to grow up. 'you are now a dad, and for your boy's sake you need to become a man'. It was what I needed, I stopped going out with my mates, Lucky Jim had to change, and I did. Before I was part of a big family, but now Tony has arrived, I am a 'family man' with responsibilities to me and mine. I do not think I could find the exact words to describe the way I felt, holding my baby boy, I was proud, happy, and excited all at the same time. Fighting not with my fists but with my emotions that had flooded over me making me feel sick with joy.

Round 5

The Family Man

That summer I 10 fights and won them all. 76 seemed to be on us in a blink of an eye. That eye would prove to be a problem. I got to fight number eight when I lost to Peter Cain, again getting stopped because of my eye injury. If you have a weak spot the boxing game will high light it for you. Of course, my opponents knew about my re-occurring eye problem, they were professionals like me, and I would expect their managers to give them all the information needed about me as that was one of the keys to success. Knowing your opponent, how he moves his history but most of all his weak points. I was boxing much better, dad was right, my lad Tony seemed to give me a sense of responsibility that I had always lacked before becoming a dad. I was to fight a boxer called Kevin White. In the dressing room, I felt a bit rough, when I got home I was being sick down the toilet, I had flue, but despite this handicap I still beat him. Maurice Hope, who was the European champion, vacated the British title so I was set to go for it. They matched me against an old foe, Albert Hillman, I remembered him, and the fact I beat him as an amateur. These things are important, how confident you feel is a big part in the winning process. He would also know that I had beaten him. This, hopefully, would give me an edge, and the belief that if I had 'done him' once I could 'do him 'again. He came from Orpington, sort of South London v East London.

The British Light Middle Weight title, win against a man you have already beat, and they crown you champion. This was what I ran the roads before dawn for, spared for hours and fought all the way to this dressing room. I had trained harder for this fight than I have ever trained before. It was not some Poxy back street gym this was the Albert Hall. My dad had worked his socks off getting the coaches from the Island to give me plenty of crowd support.

Tuesday 1st of February 1976.

As I walked from the dressing room the anthem played and the crowd made a giant wall of sound that made my hair stand on end. I was so proud I felt like I was walking on air. Everyone has dreams, but when those dreams come true to the sound of a roaring crowd and the national anthem, it was almost beyond belief. The feeling gave be the biggest 'buzz' I had ever experienced. From my corner, I could see my dad, and the pride in his eyes bought a lump to my throat. My engine was running, and I was more than ready. The bell went, and I came out of my corner like a rocket. I put pressure on Hillman from the first punch, I continued pushing and crowding him, never giving him a chance to get himself together. From the side of the ring I could hear my manager Terry Lawless shouting at me not to get over excited, but I had the 'bit between my teeth' and I had no intention of letting up. By the 7th round it was all over Hillman had had enough and the title was mine. My dad was in the ring with me, the noise so loud he had to shout in my ear to make himself heard.

He put the belt round my waist and all my Christmases came at once. This feeling stays with me today, I would like to have frozen the moment to allow me to go back in time and re-live the feelings. We went from the Albert Hall to a local pub on 'the Island' the Robert Burns. The crowd that cheered me win, now all begged to buy me a drink

I felt like I was the king of the world, I remember every punch and the feeling as the crowd cheered and called my name. It was this moment that made all the training and early morning runs worthwhile. I was now 'the champion' that was official . I took the praise from friends and family and wanted the night to slow down, to soak up every, last drop, of excitement. The look on my dad's face said it all, I was in boxing heaven.

Three weeks later I box a decent fighter from Philadelphia called Jimmy Savage. He put me down in the first, and I supposed the crowd thought 'this won't last long'. But I got up put him down with the next punch, then stopped him in the 2nd. The crowd were on their feet screaming with delight, after thinking I was about to lose, then giving it back double and finishing him off in the 2nd they were delighted. A month later I am back. This time fighting a good seasoned boxer from Basingstoke called Trevor Francis. He was a tough nut to crack, I finally beat him in the 10th. I then took on a good French fighter called Michael Chapia, who I stopped in the 9th. Then Julio Garcia from Puerto Rico, this time I stopped him in the 10th. was only 21 and getting so much valuable experience. Now I had the title the time had come to defend it. My opponent was to be former British title holder Larry Paul. He was a good fighter, beaten by Maurice Hope, world champion and Alan Minter World Middle Weight Champion.

This was his chance against the young title holder of the British Middle Weight belt. It was always going to be tough, again I increased my training, I had seen him fight, it was October and I did not want to lose what I had fought so hard to get. At the weigh in Larry looked very confident, but when I looked his in his glaring eyes I saw the real value of his challenge. The nerves I had before were now turned into positive vibes, I was not going to lose. The crowd were up for it, despite the noise I could still hear my cousin, Ronny

Bender jnr, screaming my name and urging me on. He had told me the prison had supplied a radio so his dad, who was doing 20 years, could hear his nephews fight. I have the fights on DVDs and you can quite clearly hear my cousin to 'go on Jimmy, 'give him one'! always bring a smile to my face when I watch them back. The 3rd round was mayhem. I had him on the ropes, he was almost falling through them, and I kept hitting him. He caught me with a few punches that made me dizzy and reminded me to box clever. But in the next round, the 4th, I had him, the few punches he threw before, that caught me, was my wakeup call, so I let him have in the fourth and the fight was stopped.

And my future was looking brighter with each fight. My Theresa had her second baby Cortney. I was now the father of two boys, life was sweet. I went for a job a few hundred yards from where we live for the council at Popular baths as a handy man. You needed to have a few skills in building and DIY, the bloke that interviewed me asked

'what makes you think you're a handy man?'

I replied (cheeky as ever) because I only live around the corner'

He was quite for a bit and I thought I had 'made a balls up' (got it wrong), then he burst out laughing and gave me the job, Lucky Jim wins again.

Having a day job and getting money from the fights meant we could start looking for a house to buy instead of renting from the council, not bad for a couple of kids from the back streets of the Isle of dogs. I had two more fights at the start of 78. The first was Clarence Howard from Arizona, I stopped him in the 4 rounds. The second was with A French boxer, George Warusfel, the French Champion, who I beat on points. They now talked of me defending my title to win the Lonsdale Belt outright. As I was now training full time, I could come down a weight. I could go down to Welter Weight, a weight I always felt was my true weight. I found the light middle Weight boxers were always bigger than me. Terry spoke to me about a possible fight with Dave 'boy' Green. I agreed with him Dave-boy was a strong boxer and I would relish the challenge. Then he mentioned John H Stacey who had beat Warusfel, the French Champion after I did. But John H was a good and loyal friend and not the power house he used to be. I told him I could not do it, it would be like boxing one of my own family. He understood, boxing with such an emotional handicap would make an advantage for my opponent. Terry was a good business man and fighting John H with the way I felt did not make good business sense. The match against Tony Pool was brutal I won but the damage I done meant Tony had to hang up his gloves he never fought again. That meant I now not only had the Lonsdale Belt but now owned it outright. The Dorset Arms in Millwall was the celebration and adulation of the belt and its young owner. Seeing my dad looking so proud of his boy was one the best feelings of my career. I was due to go on television the next day but had to be rushed to the hospital to re-fix my broken nose. It was a very bad break and needed a long rest to heal properly. Many years later, looking at my old records the doctors discovered it was the damage done in this fight that gave me a small brain seizure, that would end my boxing career. A week into my recovery I get and award for the best fight of the season with Tony Pool. Presented at Wembley by Maurice Hope. It may well have been the best fight for the fans, but it was Tony Pool and Jimmy Batten who paid the biggest price with the damage to our bodies. But the roaring crowd at Wembley, the warm hand shake from the great Maurice Hope, and bathing in the spotlights, pushed any doubts about fighting to the back of my damaged head. Maurice was vacating the Euro title and my Manager Terry Lawless matched me with a Frenchman named, Chilbert Cohen. It sounded great, but my nose was not fixed so I could not spar in case it got as knock and broke again. If you do not spar you cannot stay sharp, a match against an opponent who is evenly matched would need that sharpness, to have 'the edge'. Having the edge was all it took as at this level a match could be over in the blink of an eye. One false move and you could go down. When this happened to my opponents over the years, I would go in as soon as he got up. Before he could gather his thoughts, I would finish him off. It's this 'killer instinct' that makes champions. 'As soon as you see the opening get stuck in and get it done'. Words of wisdom that stuck with me throughout my time in the ring. Should I take the chance, my management said yes, but it would be me standing in front of a very good French hard hitter not them. The papers all said I would get £17,000 for the fight. This was a lot of money and would have cleared off my mortgage plus giving me the Euro title. But the Tony Pool fight had done more damage that my busted nose, apart from the fact I could not spar in training, I did not feel right, I had no 'fire' in me. My dad took me aside and told me 'if you don't feel right boy you should not fight'. But my manager disagreed, and he had got me this far, so I agreed to fight. Terry said your Pressure will stop the fight in a few rounds. He was right he knocked me out in the third. With trying to protect my nose and no fire in my belly it was the Frenchman that saw the opening and finished me off as I had done to many of my opponents in the past. I did not get 17 grand (£17,000) I only got £5500, I say only, it was still a lot of money, but as it turned out this was a fight too far and the biggest mistake my management and 'Lucky Jim' made.

78/79 I boxed and beat Audra Love, a very good fighter, of Texas then straight on to stop Dave Proud, of Penge, in 6 rounds. My next fight is in the Monti Carlo, just before the fight I had a match with Colin Ward of Northampton beating him on points. I got a bad cut over my eye in this fight so had to pull out. It was a pity, I liked Monti Carlo and had been earlier that year to watch Carlos Monzon defend his world middle weight title. Alan Minter also boxed a great fighter, in his day, and former world champion Emile Griffith.

But every cloud has a silver lining and every sport has its king. The greatest showman of all time, Muhammad Ali, was in the UK and we had been invited to a dinner function where he was the guest of honour. When he walked in with his wife the crowd started to clap. They say he lit up the room, he certainly got all the attention, the UK loved him. I had gone with Theresa and my mum and dad. He came over to our table and had a chat, he was a very likable giant of a man. Within a few minutes he had us all laughing. He told me he was keeping a special eye on me because I was too good looking, and his wife fancied me. I took to him straight away. The boxing world was angry and shocked when, after this man had won them gold medals in the Olympics for his country and won the world heavy weight title, the American government, who were desperately trying to get more young men, the average age of a soldier sent to Vietnam was19, to sign up to fight in the US army. They needed to make an example and took away his titles for refusing to fight in the Vietnam war. "I have nothing against the Vietcong" he said. Amongst the boxing community they all felt this was an outrage, Boxing is one against one. You have no team mates to support you, what you win in the ring should only be taken away in the ring. What a man believes should not be part of a decision of who holds the title. In Feb 6th 67 they stripped him of the world heavy weight and ABA titles. Due to world - wide condemnation of this unfair act Ali got the ban lifted in 1970. But, as with me, the upset had its effect. He fought Joe Frazier in 71, this was considered the fight of the century and the first time Ali lost. But he was back where he belonged. We had a great night and meting him is a memory that I will never forget. My dad said I was not training as hard as I used to and seemed a lot slower. I increased my training and tried hard to 'freshen up'. Theresa had our third child on our wedding anniversary, a boy we named Jimmy (Jim boy) we now had three boys and I was chuffed (very happy)

September 11th, 1979; For my next match, I am fighting Pat Thomas the former welter weight Champion. For the defence of my title. I was training hard and a week before the fight I was sparing with the North East Light Heavy Weight Champion named Johnny Waldron. He was a lot heavier than me but was hitting lighter, he caught me a lucky blow on the chin, it made me dizzy, unusual when you are only sparing, and I wobbled quite a bit. Looking back, I now know it was that moment I lost my confidence. Terry should have pulled me out of the next fight, it felt like it was not me getting in the ring, my confidence was shattered. Terry was a good manager, but this time he made a mistake.

Waldron won the fight, but I felt I had done enough to win it.

In the dressing room, I had a sponsor's name on my shorts, the BBC, who were to televise the match, told me to remove the sponsor's name or wear different shorts. I was getting very frustrated. I should be psyching myself up for the fight, not arguing about my shorts. Then they changed their mind and said I could wear them, I just felt like telling them all to fuck off out of my dressing room and give me some peace. I lost it and told them I am not fighting. My trainer Frank Black talked me back into fighting. The second round, Pat Thomas head butted me, the fight should have been stopped there and then but the ref said, 'fight on'. I had a giant lump on my head and by the 9th the bruise from this head butt had spread all the way down to my chin and I could not see straight. I take nothing away from Pat Thomas he was a good fighter, had it been the real me in that ring things may have been different, but it wasn't. In the hospital, they put me on a machine to ease the pain, but it did not make the pain any more bearable.

In December of 79, At Wembley Stadium I fought George Walker of Tottenham, and beat him on points over 8 rounds.

But now the problem was money, having lost my title the fights were not paying anywhere near what they paid when I was champion. I have 3 sons and a mortgage and do not earn enough at work to pay my bill. Theresa was a legal secretary but with 3 boys to look after she could not return to work. It was down to me. Christmas was a tough time, so I made the decision to turn to crime to try to get the bills paid. My mates were into all sorts, credit card theft, stolen goods and robbery (so I am told). I bought myself a van and became a delivery driver that asked no questions. They were not the brightest bunch, my mate kipper told me he was to rob a tobacco shop and needed my discrete services, as he was to enter through a skylight window he would need a quick get-away. But it never happened, it rarely went to plan. The way I saw it if they put as much effort and thought into their crime as I did to win a fight they may have been more successful. I got the message that the place had been robbed the week before, so they bricked the window up, and Kippers 'window' of opportunity never turned up and neither did the cigarettes. You are only called a thief if you get caught, if you are successful you are called a business man. Right now, my business was going through a rough patch. There was the odd bonus I was delivering a load of kettles that may or not be stolen, I was told they were fire damaged stock. I delivered them to a warehouse and got the signature of the Chinese man in charge. It was in a remote area of a trading estate, two days later they were still outside the building. Somebody told my mates who went and stole them back.

I had 3 more fights that year against one Charlie Malarkey of Glasgow, I stopped in 4 rounds another was Wayne Barker, former Middle Weight Champion, who also was stopped in the 4th.

1981. I was not doing the training I done before, I would miss out on the running and not work as hard in the gym. I need someone to 'push me' and believe in me. On March the 7^{th,} that year I boxed Bill Wraith of Cardiff winning on points. May 81 and I was not getting the regular fights that I used to get as champion. It was not a good thing, as they did not pay enough to cover my bills, I needed the income from my van business I call Deals on Wheels. On May the 26th at York Hall, I fought Chris Christensen of Stoke Newington, and because of my lack of training, and my mind being elsewhere, I lost, it was close call, but I knew, and my manager could see, I had lost my 'spark', that killer instinct that had been so successful in the past wash now a shadow of its former self. Terry Lawless told me that night it 'was time for me to retire'. I was very confused, boxing was all I ever knew from a child. But my days on the street 'ducking and diving' would not last forever. Each time you took a risk the chances of failure increases for the next time, I was as carful as I could be to ensure Deals on Wheels did not 'get a puncture' but my mates who I was doing business with did not have the responsibilities I had, so getting caught was not 'if' but when.

After the second world war, my Aunt Eileen married an American soldier. My nan would often go over to visit and sometimes they would come to the UK. My uncle George, Aunt Eileen's husband was a successful builder. Some of my other uncles had gone out to work for him in the past. His company built the Seers Tower, which was, in its day the tallest building in the world. On his last visit George told me he could get me work in the USA and the wages were much higher there than they were here. So, I made the phone call and arranged a visit. I was going out there on my own, leaving Theresa and my boys for 6 weeks, which was not going to be easy. I went in June, George and Eileen lived in a luxury bungalow in Midlothian, just outside of Chicago. It was great to meet them and my uncle John who had moved out earlier in the year. The president of Morse Diesel, that they both worked for, was very close to George, having both been with the company for some time. He became good friends with me from the start. George introduced me to many powerful people. There was Ed Kelly, head of the powerful

Chicago 81 left to right Gene Kelly Terry Martin me Tony Zale Uncle George and Ricky Cantaloupe

Chicago Park District, and the great Jim Martin who seemed to oversee the whole of Chicago. Jim would sit in a restaurant and whilst we were talking people came up to talk to him all day long. Jim's son Terry also worked for the company became a good mate. One weekend I stayed at their house and we went to see Neil Diamond singing at the Chicago Arena, he opened with 'Coming to America'. It sounded like he was singing to me. His mum and his family were good to me and I took to them straight away. Ed let me train in the Fuller Park Gym, that was in the south of the district. The Gym was in the black area of town. At time, and even today, Americans were very prejudice. I did a lot of sparing in the gym and all the locals wanted to take me on. The atmosphere was great, we were as much family, despite the colour difference, as we were on the Isle of dogs back home. George took me regularly to the gym and played a big part in my life and inspired me to put down my story on paper. I would work down the river front as a labourer, but was not given that much work. Whilst staying there my Uncle George arranged a trip for us all. My Aunt could not come as she suffered brain aneurisms and was unwell. But Ray Worley, the company's president, Jim Marin and my old china (china plate, mate) Terry Martin made the trip to see Count Bassey. He was very old, but it was a great show. After I had been there for 4 weeks they told me I could come back and have a job whilst continue to box. They got me a union card and helped me out with my visa.

George and Eileen helped me pay off some of the debts, gave me 2000 dollars to 'tide me over', with what I saved I figured we would be okay.

So, home I went and asked Theresa if she would mind starting afresh in America. Our parents backed me up and said we should make the most of the opportunity. We would have to sell out house, find somewhere in the US to live, find a school for Tony. We thought about renting our UK house out, I sold my car and 'deals on wheels' to pay for the fare. We had so much to sort out. Theresa said yes, so we are off to a new life and a new career on the other side of the 'pond'.

Just when it was getting a bit 'dodgy'(risky) on the streets of the East End, and the pound notes were thin on the ground, the opportunity for a fresh start, and a new career drops in lucky Jim's lap.

So, it's decided, after a bit of persuading, that the Batten family should move to the United States of America. Theresa did not want to rent the house out and we could not sell it as a friend of ours, Peter Stapleton, was putting wooden beams on the outside of the property. He would stay in the house whilst the work was carried out. But we would still have to pay the mortgage payments and had no guaranteed income coming in. So, we had problems from the start. Saying good bye to my good friends down the gym was harder than I thought. They bought me a very good pair of trainers, or sneakers as my new neighbours would call them, as a 'going away present'. When Bert Lyne, a very good friend to us both, brought them round it was like having to realise there was no turning back. Theresa was upset, and so was I, but I was also excited about the great adventure we were about to go on. We were going to leave family and friend and live thousands of miles away. Whilst our families were not happy about us re-locating they all were behind us as they saw the opportunity for us to have a better life. I needed to go out first and find a place for us to live. As I had a fight booked for October with the promoter Ernie Terrell, former heavy weight champ who lost to Muhammad Ali, I left in September. This would give me time to find a place for us all and put in some extra training. I was a bit worried about Theresa finding her way through the airport with three young boys, and all the luggage. When I left I could see the problems of other families trying to 'heard' a young family through the airport check- ins and on to the plane. It was hard enough for me. My mum and dad came to see me off and we were all 'choked up' (emotionally upset). I can still remember the tears flooding down my mum's cheeks and the sadness in on my dad's face. He had been with me every step of the way and now he had to let go and allow someone else cheer from my corner. It would be strange for me not to have family members in the crowd. Seeing the sadness in my mum and dad's eyes really was depressing. At that stage, it was not sure if this was goodbye for now or goodbye forever for their grandchildren. But they knew I had to give it a go, it would be a great adventure for the 5 of us. Once on the plane my thoughts were of the future. With the on- board film (movie) and hot meal I began to relax. My Chicago friends and contacts had sorted out my visa and a union card. With the union card, I could get the insurances needed including medical insurance. When I landed the airport, the customs people did not like the papers they had got me. It took 6 hours before I was cleared to go through. My uncle George and his friend called Ricky Cantaloupe waited patiently on the other side of the barriers. It was Saturday and the sun shone down on the great city as they drove me home to see my aunt Eileen and her adopted daughter Barbara -Ann. They gave me my own bedroom and I started right away looking for a flat so my family could join me. Every morning at 6 am I went for a run around Midlothian. I used to run past the army barracks and became friends with some of the soldiers who would run with me. When I got back for a shower and breakfast George would drive me to my day job.

The first Monday with drove along Lake shore drive, the view was fantastic. On site, all the crew were more than friendly. The big attraction was the way I spoke, they used to try to mimic my London accent, it was a great laugh. Especially when they did not understand me. or when I used the English version of their American words. The problem was I was not given a lot of work to do and I get bored very easily. George said he caught me once leaning on my broom fast asleep.

At 2pm George would return to take me to the gym. It was tough, being a former British Champion, everyone wanted a 'piece' of me. So, whoever I spared against went in hard and tried to be the one who knocked down the British Champ. I had to be on my guard all the time. A trainer wanted me to spar with his boxer, so I said yes. He ran straight at me and started to kick me. I complained to his trainer and he said it was okay because his boy was a kick boxer. So, I elbowed him in the eye and it started to bleed. The trainer jumped in the ring very angry and shouting. He took a swing at me and, by then I had taken off my gloves, so I hit him full on the chin. He hit the floor with a loud thump. HE JUMPED UP AND RAN OUT OF THE RING. I THOUGHT THAT WAS THAT, BUT HE HAD GONE TO HIS DRESSING ROOM AND GOT A GUN! He came charging back up the stairs with the intention of shooting me but was stopped my other gym members who, held him back, and bustled him away to give him time to calm down.

I was beginning to see the difference between the UK and the USA. If you piss someone off here they wanted to shoot you, and since most homes and many people had a gun this happened many times every single day. There were things you did and things you did not do. Whilst training in the ring a few weeks later a white trainer and a black trainer was arguing by the side of the ring. The white trainers friend came over to help and a fight broke out 2 whites against a black. I jumped down and said to the white guys let's make it 2 on 2 and knocked one of the white guys out. The other white trainer asked me why I would take the side of a black when I was white. I replied because it was 2 against 1 and I did not think it was fair. This was a big turning point; all the black boxers began to talk to me, telling me to change trainers. It would seem, that white people, helping black people did not happen that often. I changed my trainer and my new one was a guy called 'kid' Casey, whose real name was Haywood Young. It turned out he was just what I needed, a good trainer who knew how to get the best out of me.

Joe Frazier me and Jumbo Cummings USA 1981

George helped me find a 2- bedroom flat that required a deposit, George helped me with this as well. Now I had to get some furniture. I bought a settee which was okay neither of us liked using second hand stuff, but it will have to do for now. I had a result with the TV, it was broken they said, so I could have it for $20. I could see it just needed a wire repair job, once this aerial lead was fixed it was fine. I had a meeting with Jim Martin and mentioned I needed beds. He made a phone call to a big hotel chain and the next morning I took delivery of 3 single beds and a double. In this case Chicago was a lot like the East End of London. It was not what you know but 'who' you know that gets results. I was so lucky to be getting so much help. A week before Theresa and the boys come over I ring her to tell her the flat is ready. But there was a problem. The day before she had watched a programme on ITV about Chicago gangsters in the 30s and 40s and did not want to come. I convinced her that was all a long time ago and that did not happen today. After a while she was convinced and agreed to come over as planned. After I put the phone down I heard some loud bangs as the bloke in the next street to the flats got shot. Good thing it happened after I put the phone down. So, it was all sorted and she was on her way. George and Uncle John went with me to the airport, I was crapping myself, this was my family and they had to travel all that way to get here on their own.

Their plane had landed, and all the passengers started to filter off through the terminal. The passengers got less and less but no Theresa, I felt sick. Then just before I started to panic there they all were, I was in heaven. Theresa did not look delighted she looked knackered (very tired). But after traveling 8 hours on a plane with one baby and two toddlers to the other side of the world, she was absolutely drained. We drove back to the flat, I was a bit worried, but she liked the place and now our American adventure can begin.

It wasn't that big, but it was okay for the time being. At first it was a bit of a struggle to pay the bills. I earned good money but the expense of the house in England, not providing any rent and having to pay the mortgage, left us with very little at the end of the week. When I boxed the money payed the bills back home. Getting used to the prices and how to manage in dollars instead of good old pound notes was difficult to say the least. We found a school for Tony, he was just approaching 6 and putting on the big yellow school bus, exactly like the ones we had seen on the tele we were quite a bit nervous, but he loved it. Having an English accent made him the centre of attention and that is what he loved about it, just like his dad. Courtney, my middle boy, was now old enough to go to play school, he was 3 years old. But he was not as adventurous as his big brother, and quite shy, so chose to stay with his mum and his baby brother Jim-Boy. I would get out of bed at 5.30 every morning and set off to work. George would pick me up. I started to drive myself, I had to concentrate on keeping right and not left. George let me use the works van and I would meet him in the gym. Life was hard, but we had got through worse and soon began to slowly get out of debt. We made friends in the flats with a couple of neighbours. Debbie and George Zarebiny and Steph and Dave De-France. George was quite a character; a bit of a nutcase like me. The first day we got there after me convincing Theresa the violence was a thing of the past, he came over to show us the new hand gun he had bought. It was about the last thing on Earth she wanted to see at that time. We had a trip out to Missouri for a few days and visited the place where Jessie James had hidden, out on the river. It was all very realistic, set in a theme park we had never seen anything like it. The boys loved it, every morning we would all go for a swim in the hotel swimming pool. But soon the playtime had to stop as it was time for my first fight. It would be the first time I had boxed in America with my family to cheer me on. Ernie Terrell, the promoter, had me top of the bill. Jimmy Batten v Jessie Abrahams over 10 rounds. At the weigh in he seemed much taller than me. I decided I would have to get in close and give him no room to use his extra reach. The announcer held onto the mike above his head and looking up announced; 'Jimmy Batten formerly London England and now of Chicago USA. It seemed strange hearing these words but it's all part of the 'razza mataz' that makes boxing such a widely followed sport. My Aunt Eileen with my cousin Barbara-Ann and Uncle John were seated nearby and in the corner, was Ray Worley, president of the company with Jim and Terry Martin and Ed Kelly, were all ringside.

The bell went, and I could feel he was a powerful boxer with a height advantage, I would have to box clever to get over this one. We clashed heads and I had a big gash across my forehead. It was bleeding quite badly, the ref, who worked for Ed Kelly, wanted to stop the fight, and looked over to Ed for the okay. Ed shook his head and said no! My corner did a fantastic job patching me up, and stopping the blood pumping out. I knocked him out in the 4th and the crowd went wild. We all looked forward to the next fight. I had to go to the clinic to get my eye fixed up properly 5 stitches and I am good to go, the money I had just earnt will clear some of my English debts. There was talk of a me going on the bill at a Joe Frazier comeback fight. I was asked to attend a meeting with a 'matchmaker' and promoter. It was a small Italian Restaurant in Tailor Street that was notoriously known for its past links to the Mafia. George went with me as a manager, but I really managed myself. We sat down, and I had already been told by my new USA friends how much to ask for. They spoke first and offered me $1500 and 5% of the tickets. I asked them if I could make a phone call and they said yes. I rang the number my friends had given me and passed the phone to the promotor. He hung up the phone and said the fee was now $3000 and 10% of the tickets, which I accepted.

'It's not what you know but who you know that matters'

I began to train hard, not sparing as I needed time for the cut to heal. About 10 o'clock at night a few days later, George was taking me home after training when I began to feel unwell. Sick and dizzy, as if I had been spinning round and round on the spot for too long. At first the clinic though it was a heart problem as my blood flow was slow, about 25 beats to the minute. That was not only slow but very dangerous. They sent me for heart tests, but they come back fine. So, it was off on the trolley for a brain scan. Which exposed the problem. The test showed I had 2 brain seizures and a leak on the brain, the leak they could stop, the brain seizures were life threatening. All this had to be paid for, in America nothing is free. But lucky for me I had insurance with my union card, so I got the best treatment available. My luck is still with me, then they tell me I can never ever box again. 'what if I did I asked?' 'then you would be dead' they replied.

Looks like I am well and truly fucked, here I am, thousands of miles from home, starting a new life in America whose major support was going to be the money I earn from boxing. Now I have just learned if I box I die, if I don't box my little family will not survive the winter. How could this have happened? It looked like a combination of things and the abuse my body had been put through over the years was now taking its toll of a not so young body. The break in my nose during the

Tony Pool fight was much more than was first thought, the smashing of a studded cricket bat round the back of my head left its unseen damage. What the fuck I am I going to do? How do I explain to Theresa, after getting her to follow me with the kid's half way round the world, that my boxing career and the money it brought with it was gone for good?

Christmas, that time of the greatest expense and the greatest of expectation for children was on the horizon. The best way out, since only me and the doctors knew the truth, was to say nothing. We had a lovely Christmas, I remember on the phone call home to mum she said they had had some snow. "Mum" I said, "Over here it's so cold you would not believe it, the snow is up to, and above, some downstairs windows, where you are its Summer compared to this!" It was great to hear them all laughing, my boys and my wife enjoying special time with our UK family. I did really miss my mum, dad and the rest of the family at this uncertain time.

We went to see Tony in his school festival, the kids loved it and my little family were happy, even though I had been told it was all over for me I did not have the heart to tell them the truth about the doctor's advice. I was back in the gym training as hard as ever, and I felt great, so I told no one and carried on as usual. I was offered a fight with a local boy Billy Page. He had lost some local fights but had a reputation as being hard. I stopped him in the fourth, I do not remember him putting a serious glove on me. But to be fair, and not wanting to sound 'flash' (boasting about your own ability) he was not in my league. But onwards and upwards whilst this was going on I become friends with a boxer who was about to retire Johnny Lira. He had just had a fight for the light weight champion of the world but lost. John was half Irish and half Italian and became a special friend who I would always keep in touch with right up to his death in 2015. I keep in touch with his two daughters. Kid Casey was training me showing me good moves which I learned and remember, he became not only my trainer but also a very close friend. I went with Johnny to see the film 'Long Good Friday' about East End Gangsters. I enjoyed it, like being back home. But a lot of the dialogue was lost on Johnny, as Winston Churchill said; 'Two great nations separated by a common language'. Johnny asked me if I would like to box Mario Maldonado in Atlantic city, on the boardwalk. Mario was a devastating puncher and Johnny told me to be careful. Before I flew off to Atlantic City I had a few nasty phone calls, people saying they would hurt my kids if I went. So, Theresa and the boys move over to stay with Aunt Eileen whilst me and George Johnny Lira and a couple of friends set off. In the hotel, when we got to Atlanta, they were showing a Cilla Black film and for some reason the music took me right back to my days in the UK, it made me feel unsure of myself. The last thing I needed before a big fight was to get sentimental.

The hotel where I am boxing is also showing a 60s film, bringing back memories. The first bell and we come out fighting, for whatever reason, either me not concentrating or the sentiment is stopping me focus, he caught me with a good punch, at first, I try to ride the dizziness but soon drop to my knees. I am trying to clear my head as the referee is shouting in my ear 'do you know where you are?' without thinking I said Chicago and he stopped the fight. I was just confused, I could have gone on, but the referee said it was over and that meant it was over. I felt deeply embarrassed to go out so quickly, without putting a serious glove on him. But now I know I have a brain problem that will affect the outcome of all my future fights. What a mess, I am fucked with a capital F!

Anyway, there was bugger all I could do about it, so once again sticking my head in the sand I went back to work on the building site. The Union was putting on a boxing Exhibition and asked me if I would like to enter my boy Tony. He was only six and small for his age, but he wanted to do it, so we entered him in the competition. The union was mostly Irish, who had no love for the English, so when they announced the name Tony Batten some of the crowd booed. I felt myself getting angry if I could have seen through the crowd to find out who was booing my boy I would have gone and punched every one of them. But he put on a good show and they cheered him at the end. Being and exhibition fight there was no winners. But I watched every move and knew that if it was for real, my boy would have won. The union covered all the insurance pay outs, in this I was lucky. Although we had many problems, the mortgage back home was one of the biggest,

 We were coping, just about. In the end, we had to face the truth, rent plus mortgage was always a step too far for us. We decided Theresa would go back home with the boys and I would move in with my aunt Eileen, so we did not have to pay rent. It was a shame, it was a long, sweltering Summer that year, after I came back from my run we would both sit in the shower with the freezing water running to cool down. Theresa said she might take up running as she thought she was putting on weight. I8 cracked up, she was always nice and slim, and she ran like a constipated chicken. It was going to be difficult without Theresa and the boys, there was a middle weight who was unbeaten called Jeff Maddison of St Louis. He was heavier than me, but I agreed to the fight providing he did not weigh in over 11 stone 6 pounds. At the weigh in he tipped the scales at 12 stone 2 pounds this was far too much weight to 'give away' so I did not want to fight. In the dressing room, I had a phone call from the head of boxing for the state of Illinois. He said the bout was to be televised and if I did not fight it would be impossible to fill the gap in the programme at such short notice. I demanded and extra $500 and he agreed. When the fight started they did not announce either boxer weight. He came out strong I used my years of experience to keep him away from my head. I did not feel, at any stage. I had done enough to win. But I did get through 10 rounds giving away over a stone in weight to a strong boxer. I was very pleased with myself, and the money made me even happier.

The subject of how long I was going to stay in the states came up one afternoon with George and Eileen. They wondered how long it would be before Theresa and the boys came back or I went over to England. I missed them so much. Before they left Tony was really loving his school at his life in Chicago, Courtney, who we called Court for short, was also beginning to settle, as for baby Jim-boy he would grow up more American than English. Since they left, my new mates Steph and Dave would invite me over as would George and Debbie, but it was not the same without my family. The phone rang, back at Aunt Eileen's, George picked it up and handed it to me. It was a matchmaker asking if I would box Roberto Duran on the 12th of November. The Purse was a bit rubbish as Duran was going through a bad patch his last two fights to Wil Freda, on points and, again on points, to Kirkland Laing of England. I would find out through talk outside the ring they did not plan for him to lose again. Six weeks before I had a fight planned in Las Vegas, Theresa was booked to fly over for the fight. A few days after she landed the fight was cancelled. As we had already got the tickets we decided to go and make it a holiday. So, with George, Eileen and Theresa we flew to Vegas. We met up with the great Micky Duff a very dear friend. He was in a business partnership with my UK manager Terry Lawless. He was one of the big men in boxing and one of the game's greatest promoters. He had handled all the greats, boxers like Frank Bruno, John Conteh and Joe Calzaghe. He knew more about the 'ins and outs' (the gossip and the dodgy deals) of boxing, than most people in the game. Micky had managed me in the past, I had stayed at his house before some big fights. When we were buying a house the mortgage company asked for an extra 2 grand (£2000) because I was a boxer. Micky paid them straight away and took the money back out of my next purse. Micky said I was wrong to fight Duran at that time, the people behind him had no intention of letting him lose his next fight, they had invested too much money in him to let that happen, no matter who he boxed. He was now in a lot better shape and plans had been made for his future. Micky said he could get me some decent quality fights and with good money in them. He asked me to think about it and give him a yes or no. I thought about it. I knew the way things were, I had had fights go against me when I knew I had done more than enough to win. I am not saying the game is fixed, but when you have lots of money riding on a judge's decision, there will always be the weak and the greedy willing to, or too afraid not to, 'bend' the rules. So here was my chance to step aside the Duran fight, and stand level with the likes of Haggler, Leonard and Hearn's. I knew I had brain damage but felt good and knew I had more fights in me, I phoned him back and said yes. So, despite the good advice, I was going to Florida to fight Duran on a later date. I was on the undercard of Aaron Pryor v Alexis Arguello. Both the main fight and the Duran fight was to be shown live on American TV and later the next day in the UK.

It all seemed very exciting. At that time, I was working on refurbishing a local hospital. I had to work until 3.30pm and then go to the gym. I had to get up at 5 am and running my socks off to get in top form. Everyone at my gym were helping with the sparing. Even the good middle weight whose place I had taken shortly before. I had already spared 9 rounds when he asked if he could spar with me. I said yes, and he came at me hard, after 1 minute he was down, by the time I finished the round I knew I was ready to fight. We fly off to the Orange Bowl Florida. My purse would pay off my debts and I had done a deal with a construction company to have their name on my robe. They gave me $3000, $1500 up front and the rest when the fight was over. The plane lands and it all the intimidation and mind games start. I, had, of course, heard about the power behind the boxing ring that control many fights. In a boxing match, you either win or lose or draw, most fights are evenly matched. No boxer would risk severe injury by boxing out of his class. So, the odds offered by the gambling companies are very short. This means to make big money you had to place large stakes. Those that had invested in, and gambled on their boxer would try everything possible to upset their man's opponent, and help secure his win. It would be pointless to threaten the boxer as if he got injured he could not fight so they would not win. But a great man once said

'your body takes the blows whilst your mind wins the fight'

So, they would try to affect the opponent's mind. They would have done their homework. They knew I was at the top of my game. They knew I had been warned but still I flew in to face the challenge. And as I said when the plane landed the intimidation began. All the other passengers got their luggage and left. For reasons I did not understand, I had to wait for 2 hours before they even found my cases they were held in customs but never opened. I got to the hotel to find it full of boxer's trainers and the hangers on of the boxing world. The hotel pool was fantastic and most welcome after the flight and its problems. It was Monday a week before the fight. Time to climatize ourselves, the weather was a bit showery but not unpleasant, and visit the gym. I drove with Kid Casey, Alonzo Johnson and the minder 'they' provided.

We found an ideal running stretch for the week and it all looked good. Theresa and an old friend Peter Shaw were coming out to see the fight. One day I get a note under my door, I saw it pop through so walked over and opened the door, but the corridor was empty. The note was a warning it told me I was going to lose, and I should be very careful as I am a marked man! I set light to the note in the glass ashtray on the coffee table in my room. The way I saw it if the people behind a Duran win were sending me threatening notes they must be concerned about the result not going their way. Which, despite, and because of, their warnings meant they felt I stood a chance to win.

I was sitting in reception a day later and this very attractive young lady walked in. My mates back in the East End would say 'she had legs right up to her arse'. She sat down next to me and started to talk. She looked like a Las Vegas showgirl. A mass of light brown hair with suntanned skin and pure green Hazel eyes. I found her very easy to talk to and very, very easy on the eye. She laughed in all the right places, then she asked, "would you like to take me to bed?" as a professional boxer I had been trained to see the next move, but I must admit I never saw that one coming. The only comeback I could come up with was "Pardon?"

"Would you like to take me upstairs to your room and have sex?" she smiled. I was now in recovery mode and realising this was another attempt to get through to me, probably with blackmail. "Look" I replied you are, without doubt, a very pretty girl, but I am about to take on the most important fight in my career so far, and my wife is due in later today. Sex, my pretty lady, is the last, the very last thing on my mind." She laughed, told me a guy in the hotel had paid her to give me the offer, then kissed me on the cheek, and left. Strange things you remember, she had the same perfume on as my wife uses. I watched her rear end 'sashay' out of the main doors, and into the big black stretch Limo outside.

We now had our last press conference and Duran, they announced would fight last on the card. This pissed me off as I had already done an advertising sponsor deal, the last on the bill will not be televised so I would lose the other half of the sponsor deal, $1500 and I had not even put my gloves on. I said very little after this and the press labelled me the mystery man. I was confused, why would he want to fight without the cameras? He was in decent shape and I cannot see why a boxer like Roberto Duran being worried. We were to learn later that he was not as fit as he had made out and he had begged his manager to give him the fight. We got to the weigh in and more theatrics, a group of Duran fans, who knows how they got in there, surge forward and tried to attack me, but as with all good theatre rehearsals, they did not get close. Held back by the extra people that seemed to be at the weigh in that afternoon. I went for lunch with my trainers when a very famous boxing promoter sat down at our table uninvited. He had a loud squeaky voice and said, "you cannot try to win, if you do you will get hurt in the ring and you will get hurt outside the ring". My trainer had had enough, no more talk, he said, we are leaving. And that is exactly what we did. Later that day I got a call asking if I was once a professional tennis player that had played at Wimbledon. I told them that was ridiculous, and asked where they got that information from. They said it was all over the local papers in the East End back home. I remembered some time ago the local press was doing stories in the summer break and I had just played a tennis match with my good mate Laurie Walker. When they asked us if we were any good we jokingly replied "Yeh, we may play at Wimbledon next year." They ran the storey under the headline 'Local boxer dreams of a Wimbledon title'. I got a better call from a promoter asking would like to tour Arab Countries with the great Muhammad Ali. The money was good, we decided after this tour, and the Duran fight I would retire. I had been running in heavy work boots, a trick I learned from Chicago, on the last few days I changed to running in sneakers. We now set off to the Orange Bowl for the fight, the fight that had I had been warned about, threatened and even tried to seduce me into taking a dive. But I am still here, and the crowd awaits. I was concerned about Theresa as the crowd was 40,000 strong. But my friends got her seated in with the English fans. So, I knew she would be safe. A letter was waiting in the dressing room for me. It was from an old friend who I knew as a junior Boxer who had moved to New York, it was bought by his mate who had come to see the fight. Later he would drop in to say hello. The rumours had got through to Theresa and Peter who were very concerned about the fight being fixed, they told me not to fight. When a fight is fixed it can result in the boxers getting hurt if the fight is not stopped when it should be. My mind was in a complete mess, this was the biggest fight of my career, the purse would clear my debts. If I walked away now my reputation would be shot, and so would my chance of going on tour with Muhammad Ali. What I needed to do was grab this fight by the throat and beat the odds and the crooked system. On my way to the ring people from the crowd were trying to knock me out before I got to my corner. They were stopped, but a bit slower than they could have held them back, again all planned to upset my mind. The bell went, and I immediately sense the power of my opponent, coming towards me with smart moves. My plan was to duck and dive to avoid his punches and later rounds, when he was tiring, steam in and finish him off. That was the plan, but all the psychology of the past week had worked. I was worrying about the ref not stopping the fight if my old eye injury opened, if Theresa was okay in the audience. Bang, bang he caught me. In the USA, they give points for aggression, so whilst he was going forward he was collecting points. Still I felt I had won the first round and a good few more, But the scoring was indefensible, even today it is listed as a fight Duran should not have won. I later caught him in the last round with a combination I owe to my old trainer Len Welham. When the fight was over there was boos from the crowd as Duran waved his arms about in a victory salute. The local papers called it a lucky result, some went further and said he would not have hurt me if he had a baseball bat instead of gloves. But all three judges gave him a win on points. No surprise to anyone in the boxing world or in the 'know' in the betting world. They said they would not let him lose and he did not. But to me I had proved to myself, I could go the distance with one of the greatest boxers of all time. I had survived and got my payday. More than this, I now was in a more credible position to go on tour with the one and only greatest of all time Muhammad Ali. The papers said I won, but the judges said I did not and that was that. I had just taken the 5th greatest boxer (as voted by Ring Magazine) of all time a full 10 rounds. With three broken ribs, that I did not know about, and brain damage that I certainly did know about. Duran was the holder of 4 titles, at 4 different weights, who was known as the 'hands of stone' and I was still standing. I may have lost but I fought well and felt good. 'They' had got what they wanted, so we all move on. I tried to train again but my ribs were too sore, so I needed to get checked out. The X ray shows 3 cracked ribs, the treatment? Rest and recover, 2 or 3 months they said. Early December and I get some sad news the tour with Muhammad Ali was off, the great man himself had been diagnosed with Parkinson's and his fantastic career was over. It was sad going over to Ali's office to get back my passport, they all worked for, and loved the great man, the atmosphere was like a funeral parlour.

ROUND 6

Back Home Again

I decided to go home for Christmas. I did not let anyone know, the news about Ali had given me a lot to think about. Ali was a boxer that avoided taking blows to the head, his famous boast was "He never laid a glove on me, I'm too pretty to be hit". If his Parkinson's was due to boxing where does that leave me? I had been diagnosed with brain damage and was a scrapper that often took blows to the head. So, I got on a plane and then a train and I was back where it all began. It was great to hear the London accents again, funny the things you miss. And there she was, my Theresa, at the door, the boys jumping up and down with excitement. Sometimes, in life, you feel good, sometimes you feel bad. But this was the feeling everyone needs in times of doubt and worry, I felt at home. Soon, I was off to see my parents and my sisters, Eileen and Connie, Tony was still in the states. It was Christmas, the one time of the year everyone wants to be home for. Surrounded by family and good friends Christmas was just the tonic I needed. I went to visit the Royal Oak Gym, Terry Lawless ran the gym and invited me to train there. I met some old mates like Frank Bruno, Lloyd Hannagan and Jim Mc Donald. My plans for retirement needed a re-think. The way I saw it I could not retire as I did not have a job to retire from! I made a call to Mike Barrett, the promoter for York Hall and the Albert Hall, he told me he would get me some fights and asked me to go and see him at his office in the West End.

He gave me a fight at York Hall on Jan 25th, I was hoping my ribs would start feeling better by then. I was sparing with a middleweight called Mark Kaylor and he landed a punch on the back of my ribs and the pain shot through my body. I continued to see a man I knew to massage the ribs, but to be honest it did not help much. I got to enjoy a lovely family Christmas, and, by the new year I felt fine.

1983; Not only am I still standing but I am still fighting. I was booked for a fight against Tony Britton from Lewisham on the 25th. He was a very cagey fighter and I still have sore ribs. I beat him over 8 rounds without too much of a problem, but I don't feel I have much 'zip' in me, like I was just going through the motions. In the dressing room after the fight I was offered a match 2 weeks later at the Royal Albert Hall against unbeaten, and later European, and British Light Middle Weight Champion, Jimmy Cable. At the weigh in, I noticed, despite being taller than me, he seemed nervous. But that could all change when the bell went. I beat Jimmy on points over 10 rounds, he was a little too inexperienced to box me at that time. But he learnt from the fight and as I mentioned went on to become very successful. On the back of this fight I was asked to box again at York Hall ten days later, even though I had picked up a cut eye from Jimmy Cable, I said yes. The boxer was Dennis Sheehan from Nottingham. I stopped him in 4 rounds. The money was very handy, but I was beginning to feel that this could not go on much longer. Three fights in under a month had taken all the energy out of me. I could not run in Greenwich, as I used to, 5 miles round the Isle of Dogs was All I could manage. Something was missing, my ribs still hurt and, I was not the same as I was before, the writing was, I felt, on the wall. I was due to fly to South Africa on May 2nd, to fight Greg Clark. I was hoping by this time I could get over my injuries and get fit again.

I went for a job interview with British Telecom for a job as a cleaner. I had arranged to start the job on my return from South Africa. Going out a week before, to acclimatise myself. A week before my flight I had borrowed a van from a guy I knew in Cubit Town. They called him Skid Brown, his first name was Mark, but he had picked up the nickname at school. 'Skid' Mark Brown. What he did not tell me. Or perhaps did not know was the van was used by three rookie bank robbers. They panicked and ran away when the robbery went wrong. The police had the registration and there was me driving it around town. They came for me at 4 am, it is my experience in the past, so I am reliably told, they do this to catch the villain off guard. Half asleep criminals are more likely to incriminate themselves as one that is wide awake.

Tony top, Courtney left, Jimboy right

They could not find any evidence to link me to the failed robbery, the biggest proof of that was if I had used the van, or knew the van had been used, in an armed bank robbery I would hardly carry on driving it past the police station on the way to the gym. Had they been able to connect and charge me, even the knowledge of a crime you fail to report gives them the right to put you before the beak (judge). I would have had my passport seized and South Africa and the USA would be impossible. As the desk Sergeant said when they released me at 5.30 am, to walk home, "Consider yourself Lucky Batten, next time you may not be". I wanted to say I am always lucky, but never back chat the old bill. At times like this you smile when you are outside the police station, I just nodded and began the long walk home in the rain without a jacket. I am sure this was where I caught the flu bug that, prevented me training, and I would take to South Africa with me. There was to be two fighters going and one manager as I did not have one. The manager was an old mate of mine, and former boxer Gary Davidson. The rule was all boxers entering another country had to have a manager, so Gary said he was my manager, which was fine by me. We fly out at 3,30 pm for a 14-hour flight, with a change at Johannesburg. Straight off the plane and on to the TV studios for a live interview. 24 hours after we set out I finally get to my hotel room completely Knackered (extremely tired). On the Sunday morning, a pretty girl is sent to my room. She said she worked for the promoter and was there to provide a sexual service for me to enjoy. 'here we go again' I thought.

"I am sorry" I said, "but I am exhausted from training, but thanks anyway" She spun on her heel and walked towards the door. Seems she does not get turned down that often and remarked as she left;

"Don't bother me I get paid either way".

The good news was my flu is getting better. Next time I saw her she was hardly wearing any clothing at all as she smiled at me, whilst carrying around the round card in the ring. On the day of the fight I get on the scales and find I am 5 lbs over weight. They would not allow this in Durban, so I skipped in the sauna room and then went for a run on the beach and got down to my accepted weight. At lunch, I picked up a food bug the gave me a severe case of the 'trots' (Diarrhoea). What a mess losing 5lbs and now losing more in the Carzie (toilet). All afternoon I was back and forward to empty my bowels. Even on the way to the ring I had to make a quick visit to relieve myself. The Fighter I am up against was at least 6ft 2inches, as he came out I caught him a right 'crack' on the jaw. He was visibly shaken, and I thought I had him. But I had enough crap going around my head, and flowing out my bowels, that stopped me doing what I should do to secure a win. He beat me on points. He should have beaten me much easier than he did. Everything I done was wrong, I needed to get my head sorted out. When we got back I agreed that Gary should manage me.

Back home I get the news that I would be fighting for the British Title, it was a dream come true. The problem I had was the secret, of my brain damage, I carried around in my head like a stone weight around my neck. I was not 100% sure I would be fit enough to take on a title challenge. Then to add more problems I had a phone call from America. Ernie Terrell, the promoter, offered me $1500, and pay my travel costs, to fight on August the 15th in Chicago. I was worried, not only about the brain damage but also my ribs. They had never cured completely since three of them were cracked in the Duran Fight last year. But the man I was fighting was Billy Page, I had beaten him easily before, so despite all my doubts I said 'yes'. When I got to Chicago I told no one of my medical state, not even my trainer Kidd Casey. I needed to make the fight to get the $1500 purse. Chicago in August is hot, not the bright sunny hot we have back home, but heavy humid hot, that makes you sweat buckets as soon as you try to exercise. When we weigh in the doctor had some concerns about my breathing and asked to check me out. I said I felt fine. He asked me if I had a cold, as my lungs seemed congested. I told him I had picked up the cold at the airport. He done some more tests and a lot more writing and then, reluctantly, gave me the all clear. I won easily stopping him in the 5th.

I say goodbye to family and friends in Chicago and head back home to good old London.

After a week's rest, I start training for my British title fight. I would be fighting Prince Rodney of Huddersfield on the 11th of October. I was not doing the training needed to get me to the top of my form. I could not, I tried but could not manage it. Len Welham, my trainer and my manager Gary Davidson asked what was wrong. They both said my boxing was terrible. They asked if I wanted to cancel? I could not for two reasons, 1, I had waited a long time for this chance at the title and 2, I had spent all the money I made from my personal ticket sales. Theresa did not want me to fight and asked me to cancel, but I told her it was too late now to back out. The last week of training Gary took me away Cambridge to work with trainer Andy Smith who trained boxers like Dave boy Green and Joe Bugner. It was great but there was nothing left in my tank. One night after a hard ten rounds sparing we went to dinner and I collapsed, I could not breath.

My manager asked me if it was anxiety about the coming fight, was I scared? I told him I had never been scared to fight and was not anxious but did have a cold that was giving me a slight problem with my ribs. Telling him I had not been leaving enough time to recover between fights. They took me to the hospital and had me X- rayed. The report was my lungs were a bit cloudy and I should come back in a week to see if it clears up or I may need antibiotics. I agreed to return, knowing full well I was not going to. But I was concerned, the weight of my secret brain damaged nagged at the back of my head. My lack of fitness and my struggle to breath all said I should rest and recover my fitness for a few months. I don't know why but I passed a church on the way home and decided I needed to speak to someone and spoke to the priest, I told him that I believed I was going to die in the ring.

He listened as I told him all my secret worries, of course he advised me not to fight, but after 'unloading' all my problems I felt better. He invited me to pray with him. I left the church feeling much better than I did when I went in. I did ask myself what stupid bastard agrees to stand and be battered in the ring by a professional fighter knowing he has a damaged brain and had been medical advised it could kill him. Not only was I ignoring my doctors my wife and a priest, I was also ignoring myself. I knew I was not fit enough, I could have called it quits but pride, not greed, would not let me walkaway.

The bell went, and all my doubts were flung aside, I was going to win! I lasted up to round 6 when he managed to find my ribs on my left -hand side. It was all over the ref stepped in straight away as the pain took me to my knees.

I desperately wanted to carry on, but I could hardly stand, and was fighting for every breath. My speech was slurred and they though I may be having a stroke. I was rushed to hospital, although I don't remember much about it. After a load of X-rays, blood and urine tests, I was driven home to wait for the results. The results from the hospital was showing Pleurisy. The boxing Board of control doctor visited me at home, and with my mum and dad took me to Harlow Hospital where they kept me in for observation. The board of Boxing doctor had lots of questions, he had to know if I had been wrongly cleared to box. He read the statements I had made before the fight. He could, if he felt I had broken the rules, take away my license to box. He decided I had wrongly thought I had a cold, as I had told the doctor in my dressing room before the fight. He, of course, gave me a bolloking about boxing when feeling unwell. They kept me in for about a week whilst the pleurisy was cleared up. The consultant who came around, to give me the all clear, was a boxing fan and he explained what pleurisy was, and what it could develop into if it was ignored. He said it was an inflammation between the rib wall and the lungs, it would be sore to breath cause loss of breath and make you tired and weak as it reduced your lung capacity to as little as 50%.

"So, when I was boxing it was like fighting with one hand behind my back" I asked

"No" he replied, "as you had restricted movement and little upper body strength, it would have been like fighting with both hands behind you back, and your boot laces tied together. Had you not been injured, and received the immediate treatment at the ringside, the pleurisy would have developed into an embolism which would have blocked your heart, with fatal results. Consider yourself a lucky man Mr Batten"

"Thanks doc" I said, and thought 'where the fuck do I go from here'?

Because it is now entered in my medical records that my speech was slurred, the boxing board of control insisted I have a full brain scan. The secret I had been hiding for a long time was now out. The scan showed I had post traumatic encephalopathy. This is a degenerative disease which occurs in contact sports. Bought about by repeated blows to the head. The symptoms are slurred speech hearing and sight deficiencies and can bring on the initial stages of Parkinson's. The more common name for this illness is 'Punch Drunk'. Of course, if I had stopped when the first brain bleed was discovered my prospects would be much better that they are today. But that was then this is now. My boxing career is now over, I am up 'shit creek' without a paddle. How do I earn a living now? Like all dads I wanted the best for my family. Not going to be easy on the basic wage British Telecom is paying me, I even get a job mini cabbing to top up my earnings, but that only brings in enough just to keep my damaged head, just about, above water. I need a new direction. Some time ago, a mate of mine, Micky Monahan who worked for the film industry invited me along to play a soldier in a film his firm were making with Leonard Rossiter about a farting man who played the trombone with his arse.

It was great laugh, micky was a big boxing fan and great company. Then, out if the blue, whilst I was working for British Telecom, I had a phone call from him. He said his film company was going to make a series about the Isle of Dogs. He said they wanted me as it was my home town. There would be a small part to play in the opening of the series, then I would stay on as advisor. It would last for 6 months. When one door closes a much better, and safer one, opens in front of me. Lucky Jim is back. I left my job with BT and entered the film business. I spoke to the producer and asked him about getting work as an actor. He was very polite, but told me, because of my speech impediment I would never be accepted in the industry as it was not clear enough for the viewers to understand, 'even if it was' he said, 'you would still need an Equity Card'. Now I understood the barriers I need to get over all I needed to do was find a way to get over them. As the filming went on I watched and learned. This was a different world to the one I had just left. In my boxing world, it was about being the toughest and the most aggressive. Here in the film world it was being polite, on the surface, and to smile, and keep your thoughts to yourself. I also made friends with the actors I worked with, like all business it's not what you know but who you know that matters. I got my lads 'walk on parts' and got a few locals jobs as extras. In this show business world, there was lots of parties. The crew and actors would party at a local pub. One night the pub manager, who was drunk, got into a row with the crew. I was the unofficial minder with my mate Laurie Walker, so we tried to step in and keep the peace. The pub manager lied and said I hit him and his wife. They also said Laurie had hit the barman over the head. The police arrested us both and we were charged with assault. Laurie pleaded guilty and was sent to magistrate's court to be sentence. I did not plead guilty as I did not hit the landlord or his wife. I was given no support by the producer. At the Crown court, the charges are read out. I am charged with assaulting the landlord and his wife also hitting the barman over the head. My brief (solicitor) said that the assault on the barman had already been heard in the magistrate court where the guilty party had been charged. My brief said it was a case of mistaken identity as all involved had been drinking and some charges had already been admitted to by others. The jury found me not guilty. The trust I had in Greg, the producer, was gone. Another lesson I learnt, no matter what the business, when the shit hits the fan most people save their own neck first.

I began having speech lessons and drama classes and joined an amateur theatre group. Got more work as security on some films plus worked as a film extra. Made friends with the actor Chris Andrews (Hi de Hi, Elo Elo and many more). We worked together on many films and security jobs and he became a friend of the family. So now I was 'in' the world of show business. This new world was not so different from the one I had just retired from. Both required you to stand in the spotlight, both needed dedication to get results. But that's where the similarities ended. In my boxing day's it was about being the stronger than the man in front of me. In this new world, it was more about how others saw you. If I knocked a man out in boxing I won, and no amount of bad press would change that. Now it was down to how you behave towards others, bad press in showbusiness was the kiss of death. The one thing that no one accepted was violence. In my old world, a 'smack in the mouth' was quite common but in this new game that relied on 'what face' you put on in public, a smack in the mouth and doors would begin to close and contacts (known as friends) would melt into the night. I had to learn to unroll my fists, keep my hands in my pockets and always, smile as if I meant it.

The significant difference, I was to eventually get used to, was in my old world of Boxing it was rough tough and 'in your face'. In this new 'show biz' world it was smile and gentle and polite, even when you are 'pissed off'. This was made crystal clear when, not long after I began my show biz career, I turned up to take part in a film at the old naval buildings Greenwich driving my brand new, and highly polished, Rover. I was even more pleased, and proud, when the film people told me they liked my car and offered me a flat fee to use it in the film. I was concerned it might get damaged, so they said they would repair any damage at the end of the shoot.

"No" I told them,

"Any damage and you replace my car"

Again, they agreed. I was okay until they started putting padding around the car.

"It's for the explosions" they calmly replied to my concerns. Now I was panicking, when the sound man sat on the bonnet I told him "Get the fuck off my car".

He jumped off instantly with a sorry. From the edge of the set I noticed this bloke put his coffee cup on the roof of my Rover, so I shouted at him across the set.

"Get that fucking coffee off my car!" Sorry he shouted back. The director pulled me aside and told me the get off the set and not come back.

"Why?" I asked.

"Because you do not shout obscenities across my set at Harrison Ford!". I left and learned, new world new rules.

I was invited to do security for showbiz parties and films for Phil Collins on the set of 'Buster' which was about the great train robbery. Buster Edwards, like me was a boxer that had decided to become a career criminal. He, and others stole £2.6 million from an over-night mail train, about £49 million in today's money. He took his share £150,000, (about £6 million today) and his family, to Mexico. They stayed there until the money ran out (must be expensive to live in Mexico?) he made a deal to come home where he was sentenced to 15 years. I made more contacts and was asked to take part in a charity football match with Trevor Brooking (now Sir Trevor) and Frank Lampard (snr). I scored a wonder goal, hit it and hoped, when the ball found the top left-hand corner it became a deliberate lob and I bathed in the showbiz credit.

My boys had begun to play football and were pretty good. I started to manage one of their teams Club St Mathews, my boy Courtney was their star player. Once again, I am 'up before the beak' (in court in front of a judge). This time for smacking a couple of blokes outside my house. I could not have done this because I was found not guilty.

During this Summer, I travelled to the Isle of White for a

5-a -side football tournament, I also picked up work as a comic. To obtain and Equity Card (the passport to showbiz work) you needed to get contracts for as many performances as possible. My first act included skipping with a giant boxing glove and pretending to fight with kids. I performed this routine at a West End hotel for the taxi driver's charity for children along with Ernie Wise. He was okay, told me he did not know where I would end up, but felt sure it would be in showbiz. One of my contacts knew the comedian Micky Pugh and gave me his number. I phoned him, and he told me he was doing lots of stag shows, and was I a comedian? Yes, I lied. My first gig was at a Chatham Working Man's Club. The only experience I had before this was at reading town hall where I needed a good drink and help from my brother-in - law Terry Fisher to get me on stage. This time it's a hall packed with half drunken men, Micky, me and two strippers.

Most of them wanted me and Micky to finish so the strippers could perform. In those days strippers went all the way, including audience participation with them. I went out and began my act when one of the audience starts shouting out. I told him to be quite and he shouted, 'fuck off'! 'If you don't shut up I will give you a slap' I said, 'come on then' he replied

I put the mike on the stand and went to 'chin him' (hit him in the face). Mikey pulled me back, 'you can't do that' he said, the mouthy bloke nearly shit himself. The audience roared with laughter, thinking it part of the act. Stag shows in the eighties were 'no holds barred, with the girls really earning their money. If you mix beer lots of men and two naked girls willing to 'oblige' it often as not ended up in a violent orgy. From this I got work, once a week, for the compere and comedian Frank Maloney who managed and promoted Lennox Lewis to become the first British undisputed world heavy weight champion for nearly a century. Frank held a darker secret than I did, he was a great bloke who retired in 2014 and had a sex change to become Kelly Maloney.

Doing the Stag Shows I remembered micky's words; 'don't try to be a comic, just be yourself and funny' he was right I would become a funny compere and M.C..I never dreamed what was around the corner.

1987 was not a good year, it was a wonderful year, with its ups and downs, of course. Show business is not only knowing the right people but also being in the right place at the right time. Some of the 'downs' I met a guy who worked security. He was the minder of Oliver Reed who was about to get married. He had an invite to the wedding so asked me if I would do it. I said, I would love to but was not free. Later I got a phone call from Oliver Reed himself, he said he wanted me to do it, but I explained I had work contracts I could not get out of. In showbiz, it is better to not piss people off. They say be careful who you tread on the way up as you might need them on the way down. I was in fact booked to go on a family holiday and was looking forward to spending some quality time with Theresa and the kids. Had I told Oliver reed I was putting a family holiday before his wants then my name would have been mud. By telling him I had contract commitments was acceptable. Even the greatest stars cannot be in two places at the same time. And everyone in the industry knew a contract was the first commitment. The next bit of bad timing was when I was in Chicago for my Aunt Eileen's funeral. I got a call from my agent telling me they were about to shoot a six- part TV miniseries staring Twiggy and Sean Bean and Christopher Lee. I had auditioned for the part, but the director felt I was too inexperienced. He had now changed his mind. They wanted me to play quite a big part but again the timing was wrong. As it turned out the whole thing was cancelled due to union problems. I went for some big films, Rambo 5, I was to play an Afghanistan freedom fighter, another big part. They asked me if I could ride a horse, I told them I had just finished a course of riding lessons, if I told you that I was telling the truth then I would be telling a lie! I went for robin Hood Prince of thieves, another riding job, this time I had the experience and the bruises to prove it. In a film with Farrah Faucet- Majors, my job was to serve her coffee. As I did this a voice from behind the camera said;

"Your Jimmy Batten the boxer"

"Ex -Boxer" I said as I shook his hand.

It was Farrah's husband, at the time, Ryan O' Neil. He told me he was making a film in New York soon and wanted me to play his double. It never got off the ground, but on a positive note I got a call from his agent telling me it was cancelled and told me he would keep me in mind for future parts. That was a good thing, having your name known to those that hand out the parts was 'gold dust'. That year my Theresa gave birth to our fourth child a girl, we called her Ashleigh. We were delighted 3 boys and the cherry on the cake a beautiful little girl. Later I taught her to swim before a trip to Florida, so she could enjoy the pool. Back home she went through a bit of bullying, so I taught her some defensive moves. They must have worked because the girls that were bullying her became her best friends

1988. Was not such a good year. My boys are still playing football and I run the team with our mate Paul England. Me and Theresa met him back in 84. He helped us both and we became friends, still friends today. He is in a care home in Kent, I still visit him when I can. I have managed to get a couple of film jobs with directors like Mike Lee. The film security work was coming in, I had plenty of work as head of security on the sets. Tony had taken up playing snooker and was becoming a very good player. He had a problem with a very large family of 11 boys, that lived near us. I went to speak to the parents, before I had finished speaking they told me to 'fuck off'. Then it all kicked off (a fight started). I got nicked, for assault, as I was already waiting to go to court on a similar charge. I thought it would be better if I pleaded guilty and get it over with. But although this case was over it went down on my record. Before sentencing any 'previous' (criminal records) would be taking in consideration as to the severity of the punishment dished out. A brief time later I was working at the London Hospital Social Club when a fight broke out. Three blokes came at me, so I knocked all three of them down, the 'old bill' (police) swoop in and I am banged up again and charge with assaulting three men. My mate Keith Mudge was working that night, and gave evidence that contradicted what the three had said. But the court did not believe him. When it came to sentence the judge said I had previously admitted to violent behaviour, and had been bought up in a world where disputes always are settled by violence. He sentenced me to 3 months in Brixton Prison.

'not so lucky now Jim' I thought, as I read the graffiti on the inside of the prison van as it took me from court to prison.

Brixton was a short- term offenders, but it was overcrowded back then as it is now. So, because of the shortage of cell room they gave me a choice. Go to an open prison for the full 3 months, that was 30 miles away, or go to Brixton for 1 and a half months, which was 20 minutes from my front door.

I chose Brixton which was a23-hour lock down. That meant you only saw the outside of your cell for one hour in every 24. A lot of the screws (prison officers) remembered me from my boxing days. I was in for a violent crime, so the governor said I would not get a privileged job, like cleaner of the wing. But the guards showed me a lot of respect, so I got the job, and its benefits, anyway. Two things you could do with when you go to prison. Wide open spaces and the choice to go wherever you want to. Two thing you could do without when you go to prison is a sense of smell and taste buds. The smell is hard to pin down. It had a mustiness, like a charity shop, but it also smelt both sweaty and piss like in equal measure. The food defied description, I know if you go down as a 'nonce' Paedophile, the first thing your guard tells you is 'get used to the taste of piss'. But the food they gave me did not taste of piss, it tasted like it was mouldy or 'off'. They get you to strip look in 'all' orifices for contraband and then give you a set of itchy prison clothes. They had been washed but you could still get a feint whiff of the previous wearer. Then the 'strange dinner'. After this you are escorted to your cell, after all these years I can still hear the cell door slam as if it was yesterday. As it turned out my cell mate had done time with my uncle Ronnie Bender, so we got on straight away. He showed me how to get through the long day, how to make tea without a kettle, the little 'wrinkles' (tricks to make life easier) and the ways of how to survive. My Mum and Dad, along with Theresa and Tony, come pay me a visit. I felt gutted for them, they had seen me up there in the ring as a winner and now they look at me in jail as a loser. The main thing prison teaches you is not 'never do it again', but never get 'caught' doing it again. I made a note, not about getting into trouble in the future but make sure I do not get caught. And, most importantly, never confess to anything, ever!

The one golden rule from now on is going to be 'If you get caught with your hand in the till, swear blind its somebody else's hand!' The day I got out was one to remember, Mum and Dad picked me up and took me home to Theresa and the family. She cooked me steak and chips and it was the best meal I had ever tasted. It was a far cry from prison food, meat pie that contained no meat just a weak tasteless gravy. I had a couple of 'hic cups' whilst in Brixton. In church one day the vicar was giving a sermon when the black guy in front started shouting and swearing. The guy next to me told him to shut the fuck up. The black guy turned around and said he would 'have' us both when we got outside. The guy next to me went white, he was not up for it at all. He wished he had kept his mouth shut. Golden rule, keep your head down and do your time. But silly balls me is okay with it, ready to fight anyone anytime. When we get out of there at the end of the corridor was the biggest black bloke I had ever seen. I got ready as he walked towards me, he said "Your Jimmy Batten, I remember you at school, I was in the year below you, watched all your fights, you were robbed at the Duran fight" Thanks I said, but I must sort a problem out. "Don't worry about that, he is my friend, I will sort it for you"

Thank Fuck for that, I thought.

When you first go to prison it comes as a bit of a shock. Like starting a new job, you feel awkward, the odd one out. You don't know the rules, when and who to talk to and when to keep 'stoom' (quite). The enormous difference, of course, is this new place cannot be walked away from. If you don't like the boss or the other staff, you can't resign and go home to bed. Here you are and here you stay until the 'man' says it's time to go. Being the cleaner gave you a bit more freedom than the other inmates. You could act as a go between and earn money for favours. Money was tobacco, and being the number one cleaner who did not smoke made me well off. They would show films in the downstairs corridor, one of the blokes had some cannabis and offered me a joint. Because of my training I had only ever 'puffed' on a celebration cigar. But this puff was different. It was like I had drunk half a bottle of whiskey and spun round with my head on the top of a broom stick. The whole room seemed round and not square with purple and gold edges. I remember trying to eat a bit of bread and being unable to find my mouth. I giggled like a kid, and nearly wet myself. Toilet facilities were at the end of each block, be careful when you go in there, most assault and rapes took place in the toilet. In my cell we had a bucket, the rule was you could piss in the bucket but if you wanted a crap you would have to wait and take your dump, and your chances, in the toilet at the end of the block in the morning. That was made clear to anyone who shared my cell, I had to put up with enough 'crap' in my life I was not going to have to smell it whilst I am trying to sleep.

When my release date came it was like all my Christmases came at once. Being 'banged up' (locked in a cell) was the worse bit for me. It sounds daft but when those big doors shut behind me and I was outside those walls the air seemed to smell fresher. Mum and Dad picked me up and we all went around mine where Theresa mad me steak and chips. It was delicious, great to be out and great to be home.

I was enjoying my freedom until I went shopping in Chrisp Street Market. A gang of boys, made up mainly of the family I had the trouble with earlier tried to hit me. They had CS gas and the father ran at me with a hammer hitting my chin. They kicked out at the pram the baby was in, I went berserk. Here I was out with my family and ten guys want to beat me to a pulp. I took the hammer away from him. The police were called and once again I am on my way to the police station. I could not be questioned as I had to see a doctor about the hole in my chin. In the meantime, the mother the father and the eldest son made statements that I attacked them, all ten of them. They bought up stories from the past, how I was found guilty of this that and the other, all lies, well mostly lies. But the old bill believed them, and I was arrested. Other witnesses who were in the market at the time made statements and it became clear that a man walking with his wife and baby in a pram does not attack ten armed men. The police charged them, and they were really pissed off. They started telling people I was grass (police informer) and I was let off because I grassed lots of people up to the police. The rule of the streets is a grass I worse than a thief. A few nights later, whilst we are asleep, Theresa is woken by a noise by our front door. I go to investigate, and the hallway is on fire. We threw water and blankets over the fire and dialled 999.

The men ran away, but I know who it was and so did the police, but knowing without proof is a useful as a chocolate teapot. The fact they attempted, and bloody near succeeded, to murder my entire family was greeted with a shrug by the police. No evidence means no arrests, and no one punished. In life, you win some you lose some, the ones you lose you learn from, remember, and move on.

Like the fire in my hallway, if it had not been put out quickly then it would have got too big to control. The same thing happened over the problem I had with the family That I had fought with and pleaded guilty to assaulting. Rumours were deliberately spread about me, and word went around. Those that knew me knew that what they were saying about me was not true. If you chuck enough shit at someone then eventually some of it will stick. People who ran the area, 'area bosses' were concerned and asked me to sort it out on a one on one. That would be me and him in a bare- knuckle fist fight. That suited me fine, I wanted pay back for the attempt to kill my family.

But this all got twisted, word got out that I was disrespecting

The area bosses by bad mouthing them saying I would do things my way and not what they ordered me to do. Another load of lies. I knew the rules, I grew up with those that made those rules. But as I said, 'chuck enough shit' and some of it will stick. The film business was going well so a man was drugged up and sent to end my film career. On the 31st of October, whilst working as a mini cab driver, I was playing a fruit machine in the cab office waiting area when a young guy in a motor cycle helmet ran in and slashed the side of my face leaving my ear hanging on by a small strip of skin. The blood came out like a garden hose spraying the front window red. He had managed to cut a main artery. One of my fellow cab drivers wrapped a towel tightly round my head and rushed me to hospital. This quick thinking saved my life, I was unconscious in as soon as I was in the cab. The police, my wife and my parents were called. They were told to prepare for the worst as my heart had stopped beating 3 times on the operating table. They must have been going through hell, they had to go through the heart ache of seeing me in prison. Gone through the fact I had a bleed on the brain, that could get worse without any warning sign.

Now, I would seem the acing and film work were finished, I was going to look like a monster. Who would want me looking like this?

And now waiting in a draughty Hospital corridor and being told 'Lucky Jim's' had finally, ran out. Where do I go from here? I had been arrested charge attacked fire bombed and now disfigured for life. How do I settle this one? As you have witnessed so far in this book, I am not the sort who walk away. When I came out of hospital I was at a loss of what to do for the best. The more I fought these people the more my family suffered. I told all this to the priest as I sat down in my local church. He said; 'In the bible we are taught to turn the other cheek'.

"Are you winding me up father? If I did that they would slice my other ear off" He smiled and said' It was not to be taken literally, what it means is any fool can fight but it takes a special man to walk away, you should consider yourself lucky'

"How so father"

"Well you were lucky the cab driver knew what to do and you were lucky the surgeons saved your life and you were lucky your wife's a light sleeper"

I told him it was not going to be easy, turning my back on something I have not done since I was a kid, I am not sure it will work.

He said; "Brussel sprouts"

I looked at him and frowned

"One Christmas lunch, when I was a boy, my grandmother told me to eat my sprouts. I told her I did not like them. 'Have you tried them? She asked. No, I said. 'Then how do you know you don't like them if you never tried them?"

"I see your point Father, what you are saying is you don't know if it will help unless you try it"

No proof, no charges made, was the message from the 'old bill'. They knew, I knew, the whole fucking estate knew who did it. It was his speciality. First, he got high on drugs, to give him the balls to do it, then he attacked with his trade mark knife and a slash to the face.

"Try it" said the priest,

"You never know some good might come of it"

He was right, the plan to stop my film and TV work backfired, the scar made me look more like a villain than a villain. The work flooded in. I did turn my back, and the priest was right, some good did come out of it. But it still hurts, even today, my stomach burns for revenge. It haunts me all day every day. I blame myself for not dealing with the small, problem of bullying in a more adult way. The thing is, dealing with problems with my fists was who I was, it was all I knew. Not getting payback did not 'sit right' on my shoulders even today my mind still feels like I have half -finished a cup of tea and need to finish what I started. But time is not only a great healer but when your eyes are making promises your body can't keep it is old age that slows you down. Now the film world and TV work has trebled. The scar they put on my face to ruin my career as in fact made it even better. If you need a villain who better that and ex- boxer with a fucking great scar down his face!

Whilst I was off work, due to being bandaged up like an Egyptian Mummy, an old friend Stevie Little arranged a collection from the film boys. He called me and asked me to come to Deptford high street, where he was running the security on a film being made there. When I arrived, there was a geezer on the other side of the road giving me 'the evils, (staring in an aggressive or threatening way). He was a bald as a coot and looked like trouble. I went over to him with my hand in my pocket holding my little mate. Since the attacks on me I always made sure I had my little mate with me for protection. I have been told many times that 'the less said soonest mended' so I will not tell you about my little mate. What I can tell you it was not a crucifix. It turned out to be one of the guards working for Steve Little. He was the actor, author and self- confessed gangster Dave Courtney who became a good friend.

I started work on the Film 'Henry the 5th' I had some sword fighting skills on my CV, so I got a part as an Extra playing a soldier. At night, we would all go over to another studio and work on the film Batman 5. We had no time to shower or even wash properly. Sleep was something you did between takes. One day when I was in the toilets with Chris Andrews when a staff member came in. Chris was shaving in one basin and I was sitting in the other that was full of soapy water. The guy looked shocked and shouted; 'what the fuck are you doing!'

"Washing my arse, I will be done soon if you need to get here" He stormed out slamming the door whilst my mate Chris laughed so much he nearly cut his throat. We were all getting ready for the sword fighting scene when some 'Pratt' brings out some cannabis. The whole fight scene turned out to be chaos. We were all slashing at each other, falling over and cutting our opponents well as ourselves. It would seem there had been a big delivery of decent quality weed. Two of us, with cut arms had to see the nurse. We were taken to a medical van. The difference between this van and all the others that carried crew and equipment was the two chairs and a small felt tip written sign that read 'medical centre'.

The guy that occupied one of the chairs, he never got up, said he was not a nurse, he just had a part as a nurse on TV, so they said he could oversee first aid. He really was a van driver, who told us his goal was to be a brain sturgeon. "You mean brain surgeon" I asked.

"That's what I said brain sturgeon" he replied as he put his glasses on his head to help him find the start of the roll of surgical tape he needed to treat his one sitting and one standing patient. Either he had been smoking what we had, or he had as much chance of becoming a brain sturgeon as I had becoming the pope.

It was very cold on set, we would light a small fire to keep us warm whilst we played cards during the scenes. I was getting a great deal of work as an extra on the films, and getting work as security. Along with the small parts I was getting I got a part at the Brentford Film Festival, playing the part of a boxer for 2 weeks. I was recommended for the boxer roll by Peter Longstrom and John Mc Vicar.

Then came an interview for Robin Hood Prince of Thieves. I was auditioning for the part of the leader of the sheriff's men. A dream role if I can get it, the scar helped, perhaps I should thank the 'scroat' (young useless waste of space) who sliced me, it was certainly pulling in the work. I got word, from my agent, on the fee I would get for the part, so I was off to book some riding lessons. I did ride but for this job I would need to ride better. The lessons made my entire body ache. I was sure the horse they give me had a concrete back.

In the end they changed their mind, but I did get the job of running security on the set whilst the film was being made.

The main problem was the set. No one was allowed on the set after the days filming. All the set had to be the same for when filming resumed. They could not afford to waste time and money if a couple of jugs suddenly 'jumped' 2 feet to the left. After sitting up all night, me Peter Ross and John Mc Ghee would take rolls as extras during the day. That meant sleep was little and not too often.

Once time John Mc Ghee and my -self were parked in the middle of this big forest. We were guarding the film set by watching an episode of the bill that I had a part in on a potable TV in the back of the security van. We heard somebody scream, we jumped out the van and it was pitch black. From watching a small TV screen to looking at the blackness of the forest meant we could not see shit. We edged forward in the dark, feeling our way with our feet. If we stumble on the set and disturbed the props we would both get the elbow (dismissed from employment). Just when we were beginning to think we had, or we hoped we had, imagined the whole thing another ear-piercing scream came from just in front of us. I don't know whose bottle (courage) went first, I will be a gentleman and say we both, at the same time, turned and fled back to the safety of the van. Two of the best security men in the film business who would take on anything, anything living that is. But the problem was we were city boys. The only thing we knew about rural England was it was greener than suburban London. I found out later that it would have been the female fox. The Vixen screams like a person when calling her mate.

Whilst doing Robin Hood there was Greek guy who wanted to run all the security and felt that if he could beat me in a fight it would get him the promotion he felt he was worth. A good mate of mine Peter Ross found out about this and showed the Greek some footage of me boxing Larry Paul. He must have had second thoughts as he never came near me again.

I began to search for more acting work. It was, they told me, a numbers game, the more auditions you went on the more likely you are to get work. In my old game of boxing it was the number of fights that you won that you were judged on.

Having a hundred fights and losing 80 of them your boxing career would be short lived. In this acting game, it was all about the numbers. The more work you got the more your name was passed around the desks of those that chose. I went for every audition going. It paid off getting parts in TV like 'The Bill', 'The Detectives' 'Rockcliffe Files' and EastEnders. I done films like 'The Krays', 'Tank Malling', 'Riff Raff and 'ladybird' (Directed by Ken Loach) The more my face was out there the more chance of a bigger part coming along.

How I got the part in EastEnders's was an old mate of mine, who, back in the day, was in the Terry Lawless stable with me, Jimmy Flint. He oversaw the advice on a boxing scene. One of the regular actors was due to fight another boxer. The other boxer would be me. We were discussing how to play my part within earshot of the regular East Enders actor I was going to box. Jimmy said it had took look real, so I told him I would not hold back. The actor nearly shit himself, he thought I meant I was going to go in hard and hit him with my best punch. If I was to do this to someone untrained to take the blow it could break his neck. He complained to the producers, told them he thought I was going to hurt him. They very nearly sacked me. Jimmy told them it was a boxing term and it did not mean I was going to hurt the actor, but it meant I was going to give it everything to make it look real. They believed me, I am not sure the actor did. When it came to the fight scene he was shaking like a leaf and sweating like a pig. I could see the fear in his eyes as he stood up in his corner. If this fight had been for real I would have taken advantage of this and knocked him out before he had time to get to the centre of the ring. When working on the bill the script came near the truth. The director told me to play as I would if it was me in the dock. I stood in the dock whilst another actor, playing the part of a policeman, accused me of being a grass. It 'touched a nerve. I thought of the bastards who had lied about me and nearly got me, and my family, killed. When the copper in the box called me a grass the red mist of anger came down. Completely ad lib, I jumped the dock and rushed towards him to knock him out. 'Cut!'. The chap in the dock ran off the set before I could reach him, and the director loved it, more brownie points for my CV. The problem was this TV work meant I did not see much of my family, the way things were going I was seeing them less and less.

1990, I got a call, from a company of Private Detectives. I had worked for them in the past and, used my muscle to collect a few debts in places the normal public would be well advised to steer clear of. They wanted me to head up security at the Bridge House Hotel Night Club. This placed used to belong to fellow boxer Terry Murphy, who boxer son Glen starred in one of the biggest shows on TV at that time, London's Burning. I took the job, it meant working the whole weekend, again my family suffered. But I had to work, you get nothing for nothing is what I was taught. Canning town, in the 90s was a rough area. The roughest part was where the club was.

Drug dealing was like an epidemic. The owners of the club wanted it to be a drug free area. To get drugs of the street was as easy as taking all the air off the streets. But in a club, where all entrances and exits were vetted by security could be controlled but never completely got rid of. I could never see why, even today, why the government did not make all drugs legal and charge tax on the retail sales as they do on tobacco and alcohol. Brixton prison would struggle to fill its cells, the old bill and customs could halve their staff and the government could earn millions more in taxes. But on the negative side guys like me would be out of a job. My old mate Billy Williams (aka 'Jango The Bomb') who I had worked with before, used to come in and give me a hand when it got a bit over the top (too much to handle). This kept the trouble down to a minimum. Even so, most weekends some scroat tried to stab me and every hour someone wanted to fight me. A guy called Barry Dalton, came over from America and kept asking me to spar with him. I told him no, but he came back at me and called me a chicken. Fucking yank, calling me chicken and his not even a UK citizen. So, I sparred with him, he was big but slow. I just kept dodging his blows, that slowed him down until he was knackered. He realised before the end of the round I could have hurt him if I chose too, I could see it in his eyes. At the end of the round they told him who I was and should have been given the decision against Robert Duran. He came over and thanked me for taking it easy and apologised for trying to 'dig me out' (taunt and torment into retaliation). He was a tough bastard, but we soon became friends. The place had a big staff turnover. Not many people's idea of a decent job is one where you get threatened with violence on a regular basis. One night, the club manager told me the compere had pulled out. The compere done a bit of singing and a bit of comedy. The manger asked me to step in. Not because he recognised talent when he saw it, but because he was desperate. I told him I could not sing but I could give it a go. It went down better than expected. A new path in my career opened. After a little while I bought in my own Karaoke and music and began seeking work in the pubs and clubs.

I was still running the football clubs. We are playing in the midweek league and win the league title, that gives my team a crack at the cup final. My boy Courtney and my mate Steve Perkins son are in my team. The other team seem a lot bigger than my boys. But my team were quicker to the ball. Their manager screams at them to get 'stuck in', so they do. My little lads are going down like skittles as the bigger team kick lumps out of them. One of my boys goes down hard and the other player gives him a kick whilst he is on the floor. I have had enough, unless the ref takes control my lads will be hurt. I run onto the pitch protesting to the ref about the latest brutal tackle and one of the other team's dad, who I knew, shouts at me; "Fuck off the pitch Batten let them carry on"

Always diplomatic, I scream back;

"I will speak when I want to, you fuck off, you mouthy git!"

He came charging across the pitch like a train. I waited until he was in range and smacked him on the nose before could reach me. He sank to his knees in the mud, jumped up, and ran towards the car park. I thought it was all over until he tries to run back through the crowd waving a revolver. Just like the states, seems the UK is going down the same path. Some of the crowd try to hold him back. "Let him through" I called. He never fired the gun, and to be honest I never thought he would. He was just angry that he had made himself look foolish. Now he was shouting in my face saying he was going to kill me. Then his mates came and led him away. If it looked a fool before he looked a right Pratt now. We have spoken since and credit where its due, we shook hands and it's all forgotten. I gave up the team after that, we had won the league and the cup so time for me to concentrate on my acting career.

The Kray's film with the Kemp Brothers

The film 'The Krays' is about to start filming staring the Kemp Brothers as the twins Ronnie and Reggie Kray. The 1960s gangsters my Uncle Ron went to prison with.

 I get the part (thanks to my scar face) along with a couple of mates Jimmy Flint, (Lock Stock and Two Smoking Barrels and Revolver) who played Perry, and Ben Mansworth (The Mummy Returns and (Gimme, Gimme, Gimme) who played Tom. I play the part of Straker. Whilst all the names are fictitious the film was so well written I could recognise some real- life characters, from my childhood in the East end.

I got a dodgy offer from a newspaper guy asking if I would say the scar on my face was from my time as a gangster. I told them I was only a kid when the Krays ruled the streets. "What about saying you got the scar whilst filming the Krays?" He asked. "No", I replied, "they would chuck me off the film" They mentioned the amount £2000, but I still said no. It may have seemed like easy money but in the film game if you start upsetting the ones who dish out the bread (money) the work will dry up and you would end up pot less

(broke) and forgotten. Long term, 'no' was the sensible answer. On set I was sitting in a van with the Kemp brothers, waiting for the man to shout 'action' when Gary asked me how I got the part in the film "Was it because you were a gangster in real life?" he asked. I laughed and told him,

 "I was not a gangster I was a boxer, and I got the part because I looked right for it" When the film was released some of the lines me and my mates had said were cut out. We still got paid if they cut you lines or not, but it still was disappointing. It always gave you a doubt that your lines were cut, not because the film needed trimming down in the editing room, but because your acting was crap and they had to cut it out. I continued to try for parts, getting the small ones, expecting more, whilst hoping for the big ones.

In between film and TV work I 'topped' up my income with work as a VIP chauffer. The thing about driving for celebs is they never notice the driver and the driver just teats them as an expensive parcel. Just if you get them there, from

A to B, on time, then your job is done. There are, as in all rules, the exception. I have met several types of people in my life. As a rule, I tend to treat them as they treat me. No matter the colour sex or religion of a person, all groups are made up of good guys and arsoles.

A good example of this was a 'pick up' of VIPs at Gatwick Airport. I was holding a board waiting for three Japanese guys and their interpreter who was locally based. I found the Japanese guys without any problems, but their interpreter did not show. We waited outside the gift shop that was the meeting point but after 30 minutes I decided to take them on to their hotel in Chelsea.

On the way, back from the airport, my three passengers are taking pictures of anything British, red post boxes and telephone boxes ect. I call over the radio to my boss. He said he would ring the interpreter and tell him to make his way to the hotel, and asked me to tell the three passengers what was going on.

"I have three fucking Japs in the back that don't speak English, how do you expect me to tell them anything!"

"I understand, I think it would be best if you took them to their hotel in Chelsea"

"No shit!" was my sarcastic reply.

"I have just had a call from the interpreter, he said he is at the airport and I did not wait for him"

"He was not there, I will drop these guys off and stay with them until he turns up"

"Roger and out"

When we get to the hotel I take them through to reception to help book them in when another Japanese guy walks up to us;

"Why was you not at the airport? You went without me"

He was a very tall thin guy who I took an instant dislike to.

"I was at the airport, it was you who did not show up"

"You are a liar, I will call your firm and ask them to send replacement driver"

I don't know whether I would have chinned him (punched him in the face). Because before I could reply one of my passengers said.

"He not liar, you liar, we get nuver terpreter, we don't like liar"

The thin guy reddened and stormed off.

"You speak English?" I asked as I remembered calling them 'fucking Japs' on the car radio.

He shook my hand and smiled "I love the Rugby, Rugby speak English so Sh'tol speak English."

Trying not to take the piss with a grin I replied. "Your name is Sh'tol?"

"Yes Roger"

"My name is Jimmy Batten, not Roger"

One of his friends spoke excitedly to him in Japanese;

"You boxing boy, why they call you Roger on radio?"

"Roger is radio talk for understood"

"And why you say, 'no shit' to radio?"

"No shit simply means really"

The next week I was their tour guide. trips to Canterbury Cathedral, shopping in the West End, where they always treated me to a shirt or jumper. The problem was Sh'tol used the English I taught him in the wrong place. When the History of St Pauls was being explained to him inside the church instead of saying really to the chap saying how old the church was he replied, in a loud voice; 'no shit'.

At Harrod's the assistant was explaining how he needed to put his name and details on the credit card slip he replied 'Roger'.

"Is that your first name or last name sir?"

I had to step in before the Sh'tol part came up.

I had to pick up a group of senior management of a famous book publishing firm and take them to Tottenham Hotspur football ground to watch the fight between Joe Bugner and Frank Bruno. Both boxers were friends of mine, Joe saved my bacon back in Holland and me and Frank used to spar together. The boxing world is a small close group and I knew the former boxers doing security on the gate. I was able to get in easy and went to both dressing rooms to wish them well. The promoter got to hear of this and introduced me to the crowd. When I picked up my fare to take them back they all had a bit to drink. One young lady asked me if I was the guy they introduced to the crowd. I told her I was. She was now looking down her nose when she said;

"So, you were a famous boxer and now all you do is drive people from A to B?"

"Yes" I replied

"What a come down don't you ever get bored?"

"Not with the job but sometimes the passengers can be a pain!"

We drove the rest of the way in silence.

Another twist in the career of Lucky Jim came when Friends of mine, Cathy and Arthur Warren, who owned the 'Royal Duchess' pub in Stepney, asked me to do Karaoke.

Although I am having speech lessons I can just about cope. The singing helps a great deal with the speech problems.

I worked at the 'Duchess' Fridays and Saturday, on the promise there would be no fights. I knew my character would have to change and it did. The first lesson was learning to 'cock a deaf one' (pretend not to hear something) I learned how to sing and tell the odd joke in between songs. I had to 'knock the Saturdays on the head' (stop working Saturdays) at the Duchess, as work was coming in from all over place.

Over next few years I got busier and busier. With all the work, I was doing my marriage started to suffer. My life now was music, I worked with a few band playing keyboard and piano. With the mike in my hand, drink and drugs flowing until the early hours I was at home less and less. When I was at home there was an atmosphere that made it uncomfortable for the both of us. The gap between us became bigger each day. I had my own chauffer, Paul England. So, I could drink and still get home in one piece. Smoking cigars and cannabis, I was rushing from gig to gig collecting as much money as I could. After doing a show at the 'Morgan' pub Sunday afternoon I had to get to the West End to do a gig at the Mayfair Club and thought I would open the show with a joke. It was a celebration party, by the boxing world, for Terry Spinks, who had just been awarded the MBE. On my table was former world middle weight champion Terry Downs. He told me my singing was good, but my jokes spoiled the performance. From then on, I left out the jokes. One of the highlights, currently, was doing the music for my daughters christening.

Hands of steel Roberto Duran and a no so happy Ashleigh

Ashleigh was small but beautiful, having the boys was great but having a girl was the 'cherry on top of the cake'.

We were going to Florida for a holiday that Summer, so I used to take her to the Island Baths to learn to swim. We went to Florida with friends Dave and Maureen Clayton. Theresa and Maureen worked at ASDA on the Isle of Dogs. Watching my daughter swimming I the pool was a delight for me. We were at the same place as we were before when we stayed for 6 weeks. Going to Chicago, flying to Florida and driving by car up to Wisconsin. Uncle George had moved up there right next Canadian border. I remember how lovely it was by the lakes. Lots of Hill Billy folk and Amish people just like it looks on TV. Sad times going over there for my Aunt Eileen's Funeral and a couple of years later my Uncle George, who had moved up there moved there because of his chest problems, and died a few years later. I flew out to the funeral, it was one of the saddest moments of my life. George was much, much, more than an uncle, he was my best friend and confident. I don't know what happens when you die, I can only hope that there is a heaven, so I could sit down and chat with my Uncle George, once more.

ROUND 7

Karaoke

My life has now taken a different direction. My Singing career was going very well. From the spotlight in the ring to the spotlights on the stage. Now my singing was bringing in an income, but not enough to give up work. It was like a walking stick that helped me along but not big enough to be a crutch to support me fully. So, I worked the bar when not on the mike. Liberty's wine, bar at Upton Park on a Monday with the owner, and good friend, Dick Byard and his sister Trish behind the bar, that was standing room only. Playing to a packed audience. It was 'the' place to be on a Monday night. Wednesday, I would work at the George. It was owned by former Leyton Orient and Chelsea pro footballer Dennis

Sorrell. We had a keyboard and drummer and backed it up with an hour or two of Karaoke. Dennis only ever booked the best acts available, so I was lucky and chuffed (very pleased) that he chose me. He owned the night club next door called Stepney's. It was from here I started running talent nights. This I expanded to a talent competition. I ran eight heats in local pubs with the final in Stepney's. I bought along TV actors from shows like East Enders, and many other famous Local lads like Gary Bushel to be the judges. I was hoping to eventually sell the shows on to a TV company in Canary Wharf, but that old lady called fate had more problems up her sleeve to put the Kybosh (stop) on that.

Jimmy Batten and Frank Bruno MBE

The finals were a great night out. In between the acts I booked tribute or lookalike acts like the Spice Girls. The place was packed. On Friday, I had a permanent job in the Royal Duchess for many years, and a pub in Kent run by former boxer David Smith. The Swan and Cuckoo in Wapping was another regular job. Late nights and even later finishes. Saturdays would be weddings and functions. Moving 'up market' to the 'Ordel Witch' that catered for celebrities with a strict dress code and prices to match. I would be guest singer and run the Karaoke. Follow this by work in the 'Morgan' Sunday morning and Monday's and you can see how much attention I paid to my family. With all the attention on work something had to give, Theresa came to see me some weekend, but I had changed, I was drinking, and most nights were party night. We began to drift apart. Relationships need to be given as much thought as any other job and in my case, I had not thought much about my home life. The boys were growing and at the stage where they would soon stand on their own two feet. Tony had moved in with his girlfriend and his brothers were not going to be far behind him. London, and particularly the East End, was changing from the old neighbourhood we knew as kids. We did not feel it was a place where we wanted Ashleigh to grow up, so we agreed to put the house on the market. We bought a new build 4 bedroom in Paddock Wood. The change from where we were being remarkable. Green fields replaced grey streets and bird song woke you and not traffic. I am not saying this was better than the East End, but change happens throughout life and we had changed. It was now about the future for our girl. The pubs in Paddock Wood, where I began to work, were a change for the better. The people did not know me, my cousin Terry Dixon had a pub there called the John Brunt. He gave me a job, on the mike, on Wednesday. It went very well, so well in fact I gave a spot to my son Jim-boy who took over the Wednesday gig. My relationship with Theresa was fading, we were drifting apart. My past seemed to follow me like a weight around my neck. I would forget things I promised to do, blaming my age or more probably drink. My head was all over the place, I began to lose my way home from gigs. The time had come to go back to the doctors. Who sent me for brain scans to tell me what I already knew. Things were bad but even I did not expect how bad they were. My brain function was 60% less than the last scan. The hospital told me I could no longer work. All hopes of a career in entertainment were gone with one brain scan. But I needed to change my life otherwise I would not have a life to change.

All these years I knew what I had but ignore it, one day it would come back to bite me in the arse and that day was now. First boxing had to go because of my brain bleed, then acting, because of my speech and now singing because sometimes I did not know where the fuck I was!

The only one at home now was Ashleigh, finally me and Theresa split up. I gave her the house and moved into a place of my own, how I was going to afford the mortgage on the house was beyond me. But good old Lady luck had not finished helping me out. The mortgage company had insisted on insurance when we bought the house, this paid the mortgage off. And after a while moved me into a sheltered housing flat. I took Ashleigh to Portugal for two weeks. Another friend of mine Tommy Burling owned a bar where we stayed, and I sang for my supper. It went down so well I was invited back the next year, with Ashleigh and her mate, for another holiday. It was around then I met Janice, who was my partner for the next twelve years. They say a leopard never changes its spots and the road I travelled with Theresa became the same path I trod with Janice. Whilst we were together we went on several holidays to Cyprus Florida and the Bahamas, where I still go today. Theresa was a good loyal wife and Janice a loyal girlfriend, I, unfortunately, was not. I know I have been a Pratt, but you can't change the past, you can learn from it, as you can see I did not. And time moves on, all you have is today and a load of memories.

I decided to get my trainers licence, I had to meet the Boxing Board of Control, there at the same time, (Luckily) was John Rooney of Rooney' Gym at London Bridge. He offered me a job in his gym training white collar workers and pro fighters.

I met some great friends like Johnny and boxer Angel Banev.

After a while my health began to suffer and made it not possible to carry on training. I kept in touch with Angel.

I done some work with the kids at Kemsing Boxing club where my grandson now boxes. Lee Bender, my cousin was also a boxer who owned a building firm. He gave me a job driving and a bit of labouring when I was short of work.

It was when I was living in the one bedroom flat, that was okay but a bit tight on room, Theresa's uncle Len Darcy died. Lots of people come and go in your life but Theresa's uncle Len was special to me, I miss him even today. But, as they say life rolls on and now I have a new partner Jackie Harsant, who is my carer as well as my partner. She now accompanies me to care homes where I entertain the old folk with singing and the odd joke. We move into a two bedroom flat in Tunbridge. We do a load of charity work which I started doing in 1985 and I am sure I have learned by the mistakes I made in my last relationships, time for being a Pratt is long gone. I go to Chicago for two weeks just as we were moving in. It was great to visit old friends, but time has moved on here too and some of those I knew have died. I stayed at a small motel where I meet Jose Ruiz, former WBO champion, who took me to a boxing match in a gym. Johnny Lira's daughters took me to Fullers Park Gym, where I used to train, but it had changed from how I remembered it. When I got back Jackie had got everything straightened out in the flat with the help of her brother Terry and his wife Pat. I knew I had changed, the diagnosis that I have Parkinson's was a blow. But with the right medication you can still have a comfortable life. Jackie's son lives in Australia and we will be off to visit him soon.

This year I went to Cyprus and done a play where I win three times and win the Lonsdale belt outright. I then follow this with a song or two, a few questions and answers and, of course, the odd joke. My son Tony, now in his late 30's has taken part in 3 white collar boxing shows and I have been in his corner as my dad was in mine. I did not really like the idea of him boxing after the way I ended up, but he is a grown man and makes his choice to box, which he loves, and, in my opinion he is quite good.

Robert Duran done a couple of tours and I was with him and we became great friends. When he came over this year he phoned me as soon as he got off the plane. We met up at Romford for his book signing

So, what now for 'Lucky Jim'. One way to look at it was ending up with a brain malfunction and Parkinson's does not seem lucky. But that, as you can see in this book, is not the way I 'take on' life. The way I have always seen a problem is it's just another obstacle in the way of getting where you want to go. The thing to do is not stand still and hope the problem will be nice and melt in front of your eyes. The thing I first look for is a way around that problem, so I can go forward and not stand still. I have had, by most people's standards, an exciting life full of the unexpected and full of valued friends and loving family. I have achieved results in boxing, acting, singing and sometimes comedy. I have four lovely children that I am extremely proud of and are all doing well. I can only hope they feel I was good dad. I have my lovely partner who is now my carer and 'hand brake' to stop

Me doing too much.

One of my greatest pleasures; Presenting fomer feather weight and lightweight British Champion Sammy Mc Carthy (age 86 in 2017) at the Boxing hall of fame awards, one of the true greats and a great mate.

Last, but not least I would like to thank the two most important people in the world, my mum and dad. They give me life and supported and encouraged me every step along the way, if I was going to say why I was 'Lucky' Jim it was because of them. With them I would take on the world, without them I would be nothing at all, Lucky, Lucky me.

Take Care

Jimmy Batten

Record of fights

Date	venue	opponent	weight	result
20/10/66	East India Hall	Ray Welham	75lb	points win
03/11/66	York Hall	Mick Quin	74lb	points lose
26/11/66	East India Hall	Mick Quin	74lb	points win
02/12/66	Orpington Kent	Ron Howard	73.5lb	points win
11/12/66	Repton Hall	Brian Taylor	74lb	points win
26/01/67	York Hall	David Rose	75lb	points lose
09/02/67	Dunstan House	John Laws	75lb	points win
07/03/67	Millwall Baths	Joe Burns	75lb	points win
20/03/67	Manor Plc Baths	Joe Burns	76lb	points lose
06/04/67	York Hall	David Rose	75lb	points win
13/04/67	Islnd Baths E14	Joe Burns	77lb	points win
22/06/67	Repton Gym	Ray Welham	77lb	exhibition
12/12/67	Islnd Baths	G. Rusby	83lb	points win
17/01/68	Dag Wdwd Hall	G Peo	86lb	points win
26/01/68	West Ham Gym.	T Willoughby	87lb	points win

Date	Venue	Opponent	Weight	Result
01/02/68	Pop Box Club	Lee Jiggins	87lb	points win
26/02/68	Brooster Hall	M. Willoughby	87lb	win stp rnd2
05/03/68	Millwall Baths	" " "	88lb	points win
20/03/68	Dag Ftbl club	G Pugh	88lb	points win
26/03/68	Manor Pl Bth	G Wood	88lb	win stp rnd 1
28/03/68	East Ind Hall	Lew Jiggins	88lb	points win
02/04/68	w/ham bx club	S Woodward	88lb	points win
13/04/68	Rochford bx club	P Dollar	85lb	points win
02/05/68	" " " "	Lew Jiggins	88lb	points win
23/05/68	OR box cob	P Acers	89lb	points win
30/05/68	Horse shoe hotel	Sam Morris	87lb	points lose
18/04/68	Lake Windemere	G Glover	87lb	win stp rnd 1
20/11/68	Finchley twin hall	P Welsh	96lb	win stp rnd 1
22/11/68	Orpington Civic Hall	J Hillman	96lb	points win
03/12/68	Island baths E14	J Acres	97lb	win stp rnd 3
17/12/68	York Hall	Steve Larkish	97lb	exhibition
20/12/68	Bermondsey Baths	John Burns	96lb	points win
07/01/69	Island Baths	Sam Morris	94lb	points win
16/01/69	East India Hall	David Coombs	100lb	points win
11/03/69	Canning Twin Hall	A Hussain	100lb	points win
15/03/69	East India Hall	S Flayers	101lb	win stp rnd 1

Date	Venue	Opponent	Weight	Result
29/03/69	Pontins Blackpool	M Swift	104lb	points win
11/04/69	York Hall	Sam Morris	100lb	points win
22/04/69	Walthamstow twin hall	A Hussain	105lb	points win
30/04/69	Shoredtch twn hall	K O'Klinsky	104lb	points win
25/10/69	Coventry	Kevin O'Driscol	112lb	points win
06/11/69	Island Bths E14	A Hussain	113lbs	win stp rnd 2
25/11/69	" "	J O'Brian	113lb	points win
04/12/69	York Hall	Joe Chapmen	115lb	exhibition
20/01/70	Island Bths E14	Steinberg	116lb	win stp rnd 1
21/01/70	" " "	Bob Greenacre	120lb	win stp rnd 1
07/02/70	Rec Cent Gravesend	Godden	121lb	points win
21/03 70	Pontins Blackpool	Chris Aylward	124lb	points win
02/04/70	Island Bths E14	K Grey	124lb	points win
30/04/70	Shdtch Twn Hall	D Jurchen	125lb	win stp rnd 1
No date	Vernon Hall	Alex Tomkins	125lb	exhibition
16/12/70	Poplar Bths	A Butler	130lb	points win
05/01/71	Loudon High Schl	B Shaw	129lb	win stp rnd 2
14/01/71	Arbour Youth Gym	Kevin Grey	128lb	points win
01/02/71	Co-Op Stratford	G Santangelo	133lb	points win
06/03/71	YMCA Wathmstw	Trot	135lb	win stp rnd 1
20/03/71	Caister HC Yrmth	R Shaw	134lb	win stp rnd 2
03/04/71	Pontins HC Blkpool	D Reid	133lb	points win

Date	Venue	Opponent	Weight	Result
05/04/71	East India Hall	G Wood	134lb	win stp rnd 2
14/04/71	York Hall	R Marshall	134.5lbs	win stp rnd 1
01/05/71	Manor Plc Bths	J Ryan	135lb	win stp rnd 1
01/05/71	" " "	R Reid	"	win stp rnd 2
15/05/71	York Hall	M Sweaton	140lb	win stp rnd 1
29/05/71	Woodwill Hll Grvend	D Wood	135lb	win stp rnd 3
18/11/71	Island Bths Millwall	S Braidwood		points win
17/12/71	Cust H WMC Can.Twn	A Hillman	137lbs	points win
No date	York Hall	S Langley	63kls	win stp rnd 2
08/02/72	Café R Piccadilly	Jumbo Basse	140lb	win stp rnd 2
04/03/72	East India Hall E14	K Ambrose	63.5kl	points win
27/03/72	Piccadilly htl Mnchster	W Endon	63.5kl	points win
06/04/72	Islnd Bths Millwall	L Peachem	144lb	win stp rnd 3
29/04/72	Manor plc Bths	L. Wint	67kl	win stp rnd 3
26/05.72	York hall Bths	R Perry	67kls	win stp rnd 1
27/05/72	" " "	M Minter	67kls	points win
14/11/72	Gatwick Airpt htl	Alan Cable	145lbs	points win
04,12,72	Pav Hl Hemel Hmstd	I Pickerskill	145lbs	points win
04/02/73	Seymour Hl W1	C Keating	147lbs	points win
12/02/73	Pav Hall Hemel Hmstd		147lbs	points win
19/04/73	Stratford Twn Hl	A Heath	147lbs	points win
02/05/73	Mancal Box Clb	M Rice	148lbs	points win

26/05/73 Guilfd Civic Cntr   S Cooley   148lbs   points win

01/06/73 Sportiv de massy Paris P Bouquet 148lbs points win

23/10/73 Mrkyt Box Clb Hemel P Morris   149lbs   points win

08/11/73 East India Hl   Kurt Biek   149lbs   points win

Printed in Poland
by Amazon Fulfillment
Poland Sp. z o.o., Wrocław